Fellini on Fellini

in the same series

Federico Fellini   AMARCORD

Federico Fellini

FELLINI
ON FELLINI

Edited by Anna Keel and Christian Strich

Translated by Isabel Quigly

EYRE METHUEN
LONDON

First published in Great Britain in 1976 by Eyre Methuen Ltd
11 New Fetter Lane, London EC4P 4EE
English translation © 1976 by Eyre Methuen Ltd
Fellini on Fellini originally published in German
as *Aufsätze und Notizen* © 1974 Diogenes Verlag AG, Zurich
Printed in Great Britain
by Whitstable Litho, Straker Brothers Ltd

ISBN 0 413 33640 9 (hardback)
ISBN 0 413 33650 6 (paperback)

Stills by courtesy of Connoisseur, Contemporary, RAI-TV,
United Artists.
Photographs of Fellini by Agenzia Fotografica Pierluigi, Rome;
Franco Pinna, Rome; Tazio Secchiaroli (Luciano's Press Photos,
Rome).

Contents

Preface

This is an attempt to reconstruct a self-portrait that was carelessly yet quite consciously mangled into little bits by its own creator.
'I am my own still-life.'
'I am a film.'
'Everything and nothing in my work is autobiographical.'

One or two major essays, whose interest ranges far beyond biography and film-making, and countless smaller fragments - written and oral - have been collected by the editors, sifted and fitted together. It was an exciting, instructive and enjoyable task.

Our thanks are due to Federico Fellini, who gave us not only all the rights to his writings but also all the manuscripts and documents which had been accumulating on his desk for some time - given half out of friendship, to demonstrate his confidence in us, and half in order to get rid of us and them.
'I'm not a collector.'
'I don't preserve anything.'
'I'd like to be new-born every day.'

Christian Strich

Note to the English edition: The bulk of this volume is specially translated from the original Italian. In some cases, however, the Italian manuscript could not be traced, and it was necessary to translate from French or German versions or to use an English translation already in existence. (Detailed information about sources and translators is given at the end of the book.)

Fellini during the shooting of *Amarcord*

Rimini, my home town

When I am taken into the radiologist's room, in particular, I feel like an object, a thing. The coldly lit room looks like either a concentration camp or an assembly plant. I am left on the trolley, half naked; beyond the glass partitions the white-coated doctors talk about me and point to me, with gestures I can see and words I cannot hear. The other patients' relatives pass quite close to me in the passage, and look at me, lying there half naked: they look at an object.

Or else in the morning, I am lying in bed with a tube up my nose and the cleaners are doing out my room, one on either side of the bed, talking to each other. 'You really ought to go to San Giovanni, first on the left after the arch,' one of them says. 'Save you 500 lire.' 'Calf, you said.' 'No, suede. Remember the shoes my sister was wearing at the wedding?' 'They were calf.' 'No, they were suede.'

At night, the passages are full of flowers: flowers, flowers, flowers, which they put outside the patients' rooms, as if it were a cemetery. The low lights: in the darkness, when you open your eyes, you see a head floating in the air, lit from below. A nun or a nurse is holding up a torch to read a thermometer.

The floating faces slide silently along the passages. Sometimes the nuns give you an injection without waking you, like an assassin hired by Cesare Borgia; then you see them, back view, slipping away into the darkness.

Often, weird images loom up at me: sudden visions from heaven

1

knows where. Once I saw a small egg lying on a piece of tulle, like in a cake shop window: a good-luck egg, intended for some special occasion. It was rolling about on a very black, spotty, breathing surface. Then it vanished. I looked for the egg again but saw only a very black wall, like the inside of a monster's mouth. It didn't look as if the egg had been smashed, though, because the wall was soft and slimy.

All the time I keep thinking of the film I have to make. [*Il viaggio di G. Mastorna*, which was never filmed.] Perhaps it needs a new period of incubation.

Once I was in the office sitting on an old couch meant for resting on. Suddenly, in a flash, tons of stone crashed down on me, an inch away from my nose, something like the entire front of Milan or Cologne cathedral. I heard the wind it raised as it fell, then the terrifying crunch an inch from my feet. I leapt away like an acrobat. The wall covered everything - sky, space, and air; it was the size of Mont Blanc. I was an ant. Then I thought that perhaps the difficulties I found in making a film were the result of a basic obstacle that could be found, dramatically, within myself. I was scared, but felt more and more, in an idealistic sort of way, that I wanted to make the film. If there was sky and open space beyond the heavy weight of the cathedral, then that was the right space for me.

At that time I persuaded myself that I might die of a heart attack because I was afraid the task was beyond my strength. 'Free man from the fear of death'. I was like the sorcerer's apprentice who defies the sphinx and the depths of the sea only to die there. I thought: it's my film that's killing me.

When I felt I was dying, these past few days, things were no longer anthropomorphic. The telephone, which looks like a sort of upturned black snake, was merely a telephone. Every thing was just a thing. The couch, which looked like a big square face drawn by Rubens, with buttons on the cover like wicked little eyes, was just a couch, rather shabby but nothing more. At such a time things don't matter to you; you don't bathe everything in your presence, like an amœba. Things become innocent because you draw away from them; experience becomes virginal, as it was for the first man when he saw the valleys and the plains. You feel you are set in a tidy world: that is the door and it behaves like a door, that is white and behaves like white. What heaven: the symbolism of meanings loses all meaning. You see objects which are comforting

2

because they are quite free. But suddenly you are flung into a new form of suffering because, when you come to miss the meaning of, say, a stool, reality suddenly becomes terrifying. Everything becomes monstrous, unattainable.

In the nursing home I am surrrounded by foreign nuns. One of them comes in at the door and says to me: 'Always writing, always writing! So much philosophy!' I read over what I have written and feel ashamed if it is really meant to be on the level of 'philosophy'. Another brings me a glass of Lourdes water every evening. 'You must!' she says, pointing to it. A few days ago she said to me: 'Now that you've emptied your lungs, you must empty your heart.' I was afraid she was talking of more injections. 'Yes, you've a great deal weighing on your heart,' she said. 'But when does it have to be emptied?' I asked. 'Whenever you like,' she said, 'any time's a good time.' The misunderstanding continued for a while, until I realised she wanted me to go to confession. And so, in addition to the Lourdes water, she now sent me an American priest, who looked like De Sica, every day. 'How are you?' he would say, and come in. 'Pleurisy, is it? Nasty business.'

At five in the morning, while it's still dark, Sister Burgunda turns up: a nun with a black veil like bats' wings, a rubber tube held in her teeth, and a great basket of test-tubes. 'May I have a little blood, Signor Fellini?' she asks, like a Danubian vampire.

At nine in the evening a nurse called Sara comes to settle me down to sleep. She comes up to me. There's a dark fuzz on her upper lip. She comes from Faenza, and reminds me of the whiskery women at the Church of the Paolotti, at Rimini. I keep calling her during the night, and she seems fond of me. 'Shall I make you some more camomile tea?' she says. She tells me that her father had mistresses till he was sixty, and kept them hidden in the hencoop, where he would go along to them. At sixty, he kept getting engaged. 'My parents consent, I'm more than willing, but my wife won't have it,' he used to say, and thought himself very witty.

After the first few days (when, after an injection that put me out completely, I felt like a stone in a sling, exactly as if I were in the piece of leather waiting to be hurled out: that is, I had a feeling that I was going to go whistling into another dimension, somewhere quite outside the nursing home), everyone came to see me. At the door I saw groups of odd people looking just like paintings by the Douanier Rousseau. I heard howls, when the nuns pulled them back from the door. I distributed blessings and stroked people's

3

heads. From then on, this illness of mine became a party. Titta and Montanari came from Rimini. Titta saw me from the door and started making a row. They had stopped him, and he was kicking out at the nuns and nurses. 'But fuck it, can't I see Federico?'

There are telegrams on the table. I make myself read the strawberry coloured ones which come from the Ministries. I feel I'm in heaven. The other morning, bunches of roses appeared at the door, as in a painting by Botticelli: roses trying to come in: tremulous, palpitating roses held by two happy little nuns. They came from Rizzoli, who had forgiven me after our quarrel. I telephoned him at once. 'Your note has made me better than the antibiotics,' I said. A voice took over from Rizzoli's and said triumphantly: 'Fellini, he's crying!' It was like the finale from *The Black Pirate*. Then, his voice broken with tears, Rizzoli went on: 'You've made my eyes swim, saying something so sweet.' And finally, he came to see me. 'I hope this illness has sorted out your ideas,' he said. 'You mustn't make the sort of films you used to, it wears out your brain, you know. You must listen to me now and make the films I tell you to.'

One morning, in the passage, I saw about ten people talking Greek and holding balloons shaped like dragons and sausages. They weren't coming to see me, they were visiting a relation who had had a heart attack. I saw the sick man lying in bed, looking pale, with all the red and yellow balloons hanging from the ceiling. Why balloons? They didn't know what to bring: biscuits, oranges? They had seen a balloon-seller and had brought balloons.

But the most important visit was from Sega. I was warned of his coming. Days before, I saw a black overcoat, a pair of lively eyes, a thin little beard: 'Fellini, how are you? I'm Bissi, a relation of one of the martyrs of Rimini hanged by the Germans. They said: Where are you off to? I said: I'm off to Rome. Then go and see that clot Fellini, they said, and tell him what a clot he is.' The next few mornings, the name Piga was always on the list of those who had telephoned. I thought it was a mistake and that Bissi had telephoned. But the name wasn't Piga, it was Sega, and he had been in Rome for three days. On the fourth morning I had an inspiration. It was Sega, known as Bagarone.

So I told the nun, who always refused to let me have it, that I must have the telephone. When I swore, in protest, she looked at me very severely, then said harshly and suddenly, as if amazed to find that I had been deceiving her:'You're not a poet.' Well, I wanted Sega, who was now ringing up from the station. 'Bagarone, don't go away, come here,' I said, laying on the agony. At school, he was top of the class, and, being clever, he skipped the last year and studied medicine. When I heard this I was pleased, thinking that if I were ever ill I would have a friend I could count on who was an excellent doctor.

Well, Sega arrived at the nursing home. I told him what had happened and what cures they were working on. He said at once: 'Sanarelli-Schwarzmann'. I thought he was joking and began to laugh, remembering the double-barrelled names they used in funny magazines before the war. But he was quite serious. 'Stay on in Rome and tell the bigwigs what you think,' I said. Next day, he explained the whole thing to the bigwigs. They listened, absorbed. Then they said: 'Fascinating theory, brilliant interpretation,' etc. etc., and Bagarone turned red. And when Bagarone turns red, he goes faintly mauve.

Last night I dreamt of the port of Rimini opening onto a green, swelling sea, as threatening as a moving meadow, on which low clouds ran close to the surface.

I was a giant, swimming out to sea, starting from the port, which was small and narrow. I said to myself: 'I may be a giant, but the sea's still the sea. Suppose I don't make it?' But I wasn't worried. I swam with great strokes through the little port. I couldn't drown because I was touching bottom. I might drown out at sea; but I swam on, just the same.

It was a sustaining sort of dream, which may have tended to restore my confidence in the sea. An invitation to overestimate myself; or else to underestimate the small protective conditions of departure that might hold me back. Anyway, I didn't understand whether I should give up the idea of leaving the little port, or whether I was overestimating myself.

One thing is certain, anyway. I don't like going back to Rimini. I've got to admit it: it's a kind of block. My family still lives there, my mother, my sister: am I afraid of some of my feelings? What I feel above all is that going back is a complacent, masochistic churning up of memories: a theatrical, literary business. Of course this may have a certain fascination. A sleepy, fudged fascination. But I cannot see Rimini as an objective fact, that's it. It is a dimension of my memory, and nothing more. And in fact, when I am in Rimini I always find myself assailed by ghosts that have already

5

been filed away, put in their place.

Perhaps, if I stayed there, these innocent ghosts would ask a silent, embarrassing question that could not be answered with somersaults and lies; whereas what needs to be taken from one's home and background is the original element, without any deceptions. Rimini: what is it? It is a dimension of my memory (among other things an invented, adulterated, second-hand sort of memory) on which I have speculated so much that it has produced a kind of embarrassment in me.

And yet I must go on talking about it. Sometimes I even ask myself: in the end, when you're bruised and weary, when you're not competing any longer, wouldn't you like to buy a small house in the port? The old part of the port. As a child I used to see it, beyond the water: I could see the skeletons of boats they were building. The port's other arm, from this side, made me imagine a hurly-burly life that had nothing to do with the Germans who came to the coast in their Daimler Benzes.

Actually, the beginning of the summer belonged to Germans who were not at all rich. Suddenly we saw bicycles, and packages strewn about the beach, and cigarette stubs in the water. We children, wearing woollen caps, were taken to the sea by an employee of my father's. At that time, I saw tree stumps and heard voices in the old part of the port.

Ages ago I bought a house for an amazing price, through my friend Titta Benzi. I thought I had found a centre, a fixed point: or rather, I thought I would take up the simple life. But it must have been a phony idea because I never even saw the house; in fact I felt annoyed at the thought of a house that was shut up with no-one living in it, and that it was there, pointlessly waiting.

When I decided to sell it, Titta said: 'But it's your home!' as if to remind me that I was betraying it again. Before I bought this house that was never lived in, Titta had persuaded me to buy a piece of land by the river Marecchia. It was quite plainly the sort of place where prostitutes get murdered.

On the evening we went to look at the piece of land we heard a fanfare of trumpets. A man in underpants was hoisting a flag. It was Fiorentini, who knows everything about Garibaldi. About Garibaldi, and Sangiovese wine. His house near the Marecchia is full of prints, flags and curios. Fiorentini, who always wears underpants, was gleaming in the darkness that evening, with his face like a china puppet. 'I see a nice-looking chap, but I don't

6

know him,' he said. 'What d'you mean, don't know him?' said Titta.
'It's Fellini!' 'Fuck me . . .' said Fiorentini. Then, straight away: 'I've
found a Sangiovese. You must try it.' He is a wine expert, rather
aggressively so, and scolded me for not warming the glass with the
palm of my hand. 'Come on, Fellini,' Titta went on. 'Come and live
in these parts!' 'That way, we can go fishing for mullet together,'
Fiorentini said confidently. The Marecchia, in that part is less
depressingly dreary, and shows its stony bed. But Titta advised me
to take the piece of land. 'Just you wait,' he told me. 'The motorway's coming along here. The land'll go up in value.' Then the
motorway went another way, Fiorentini's offering me 500,000 for
it today, and the land is still mine.

The first time I went to the Marecchia I was a child. We had
played truant from school. I had followed Carlini. On the river
bank there was a black police car full of policemen, who climbed
down into the river-bed like toads. Low clouds were hanging round
the dead branches of the trees. We got to a spinney of poplars,
where there was a hanged man, already guarded by another two
policemen. I didn't really know what it was all about. I saw a fallen
shoe, the instep of the shoeless foot, and a pair of dirty, patched
trousers.

The house at Rimini. I remember the houses I lived in well, except
for one: the house I was born in, in Via Fumagelli. When I was seven,
one Sunday afternoon, we were going for a ride in the carriage. In
winter the landau was closed. Inside there were six of us: my parents,
my brother and sister, myself and the maid, all bunched together in
the dark, because we had to keep the window shut to keep out the
rain. I could see nothing. Only my parents' faces in the dark. It was
a great joy, then, to sit up beside the coachman because you could
breathe up there.

That Sunday afternoon the carriage turned up a wide road we
had never been along before. My father said: 'You were born there,'
and the carriage drove past.

The first house I remember properly belonged to a man called
Ripa. It is still there, on the Corso. Our landlord was always dressed
in blue: blue suit, blue bowler, big white beard like a divinity to be
pacified, not annoyed. My mother would dry her hands and say:
'Children, keep quiet, here's Signor Ripa.' Then the big old man
would come in. One morning I heard mooings, long complaining
cries. The courtyard was full of cattle and donkeys. Maybe there

was a market or a sale, I don't know.

Think of Rimini. Rimini: a word made up of sticks, of soldiers in a row. I cannot make it objective. Rimini, a nonsense story, confused, frightening, tender, with that great breath of its own and its empty open sea. There, nostalgia becomes cleaner, especially the winter sea, the white horses, the great wind, as I first saw them. Another house of ours, that is another house we lived in, was near the station. There, I think I had an inkling of what was to come. It was a small house with a front garden and a large vegetable garden behind that ran up to a huge building - a barracks, a church? - on which was written in white letters in a semicircle: Rimini Th . . tre. Two letters were missing, fallen out and lost. As the kitchen garden of our house had sunk, the land on which the building stood, beyond the garden wall, seemed higher than ever, way up above me.

One morning I was in the back garden building an arch with a stick when I suddenly heard a rumbling sound. It was the noise of the theatre's huge rolling scene-door being raised. I had never noticed it before. Finally a great black opening appeared. In it were a man wearing a beret and a mackintosh and a woman knitting. 'The murderer must have come in through the window,' said the man. 'The window's shut,' said the woman. 'Sergeant Jonathan found signs of a forced entry,' said the man. Then he turned to me in the garden: 'Are there any figs on that tree?' 'Well, I don't know,' I said. They were the Bella Starace Sainati company, rehearsing Grand Guignol.

The man helped me to climb up into the dark den. I saw the gilded boxes, and, right over me, the belly of a railway engine hanging from the flies, among red, white and yellow gels.

It was the theatre.

Then the man carried on about the problem of the window. I couldn't see whether it was a game, or what it was. A long time must have gone by, because suddenly my mother's voice was calling: 'Lunch on the table.' 'Here he is,' said the man in the beret, answering her and helping me back over the garden wall.

Two evenings later I was taken by my parents to see the show. My mother says I never moved throughout the performance. The train came forward from the darkness, about to run over a woman tied to the tracks, until she was saved, and an enormous, soft, heavy red curtain fell on her.

My excitement lasted all night. During the intervals I had seen the wings, the stalls, the velvet and brass, the passages, mysterious

'Dora . . . took the new intake of her house for a drive along the Corso so as to show them off' (*Amarcord*)

warrens I dashed along like a mouse.

It was in this house near the station that I made my first friendships. But No. 9 Via Clementini was where I knew my first love. The landlord, 'Agostino Dolci, Ironmonger,' was the father of Luigini, my school friend who played Hector in the Iliad (we acted out the Iliad among ourselves).

In the house opposite lived a family of southerners, the Sorianis, who had three daughters, Elsa, Bianchina and Nella. Bianchina was a dark little girl. I could see her from my bedroom. The first time I saw her she appeared at a window, or else - I can't remember - she was wearing her fascist youth movement uniform, with fine heavy, already motherly, breasts.

Today she lives in Milan and tells me we never ran away as I said we did (did I?). We just rode off on a bicycle outside Porta d'Augusto, with her sitting on the bar.

Women, in those days, to me meant chiefly aunts. Admittedly

9

I had heard of a 'house' with a particular kind of woman inside it. This was Dora's, in via Clodia, near the river. But when people spoke about 'women', I had a picture in my mind only of aunts making mattresses, and the women at my grandmother's at Gambettola, who sieved the corn. So I didn't understand. Then I saw that aunts were different, because Dora used to hire a pair of carriages and every fortnight she took the new intake of her house for a drive along the Corso so as to show them off. Then I saw painted women wearing strange, mysterious veils, smoking gold-tipped cigarettes: this was Dora's new intake.

In summer we went to Gambettola, inland in Romagna. My grandmother always carried a cane and made the men jump with it; it was just like a cartoon film. The men were day labourers she employed to work the land, and she certainly kept them at it. In the morning we would hear loud laughter and noise. Then, when she appeared, those violent men suddenly looked respectful, as if they were in church. My grandmother handed out coffee-and-milk and asked about everything. She smelt Gnichela's breath, to see if he had been drinking. Gnichela nudged his neighbours, just like a child, feeling ashamed. My grandmother was like the other women of Romagna. One of these used to go to the inn every evening to fetch her drunken husband and hoist him on to a cart to get him home. He was called Ciapalos, a Greek name which means 'Take the bone'.

Quarrels were frequent among the peasants. Three old sisters and a queer had been quarrelling over an inheritance for twenty years. They would fling dung in each other's faces, steal each other's chickens, and keep moving the fences about. In the end, after what was clearly a night spent making up their minds, the three sisters broke into the man's house at dawn and beat him to death with their carpet-beaters.

One day I should like to make a film about the peasants of Romagna, a western without guns.

There was a man called Nasi who always said: 'I can, I will and I give orders'. His legs had been broken when he sawed down a tree sitting on the wrong branch, and so he looked after cattle. This Nasi, a farcical figure because his broken legs made lop-sided movements like a frog, would start walking in that horrible dislocated way, shouting: 'I can, I will and I give orders'. Once he snatched a cigarette from Teodorani's mouth, when Teodorani was dressed in fascist uniform, with gleaming boots and his moustache soaped till the points of it stuck out like pins. 'You've smoked enough,' he told him. 'Now it's Nasi's turn.'

When I think of Gambettola, and of a tiny nun, and of the cripples by firelight, and in plank beds, I always think of Hieronymus Bosch.

The gipsies went through Gambettola too, and the charcoal burners going back to the mountains of Abruzzo. In the evening, preceded by a terrible noise of animals, a smoky stall would be set up. We would see sparks and flame. It was the castrator of pigs. He arrived in the main street, with a big black coat and an old-fashioned hat. The pigs could tell he was coming, which accounted for their terrified squeals. This man took all the girls in the town to bed with him; once he left a poor idiot girl pregnant and everyone said the baby was the devil's child. The idea for the episode *Il miracolo* in Rossellini's film [*L'amore*] came from this; and also the deep uneasiness that made me make *La strada*.

In the country, because of the gipsies, I often heard people telling of love philtres and spells. A woman called Signora Angelina, who came to the house to make mattresses (I should give a whole chapter to these jobs: the knife-grinder with his rickety contraption, the man who came to clean the blackened stove and was a terror to the maids, etc.) - Signora Angelina, as I was saying, would spend three days at my grandmother's, with full board. One day while she was stitching the cotton tufts on to the mattresses, I caught a glimpse of a casket hanging from her neck: a little glass box containing a lock of knotted hair. 'What is it?' I asked her. 'This is my hair, and this is from my young man's moustache,' she said. 'I cut it off while he was asleep. Now he's gone to work in Trieste, but this means that he'll be tied to me forever.' Another person, an old man at Mercantino Marecchia, could make sheep or chickens ill or cure them.

The wife of a railway worker who lived near the fascist workers' club used to go into 'trances'; she earned quite a bit curing illnesses. One day I managed to slip in among the old men and women who had gone to consult her, and got as far as the door of a dreary little room. An old woman with her face sprinkled with water was sitting stiffly on a chair, her back arched, telling a man in front of her whom I could not see: 'That woman is too strong for you: you must leave her.' After speaking, the old woman waited. In the end a big, bewildered man came out, unwilling to be seen, yet lingering on the stairs with his hat on, unwilling to leave, perhaps hoping for the strength to go back and get a better pronouncement from the oracle. People talked, as usual, of haunted houses. 'Carletta' was the house where my friend Mario Montanari lived. A century before, it seems, the owner of the house had made his cousin drunk, then strangled her. It was said that on some nights you could hear a gurgling sound in the cellar. People believed it was the strangled cousin putting a bung in the barrel, then in her murderer's mouth, so that he would have no peace and would be drowning forever in wine.

Romagna. A mixture of sea-faring adventures and Catholic Church. A place dominated by the dark mountainous hulk of San Marino. A strange, arrogant, blasphemous psychology, mingling superstition and defiance of God. People without humour and therefore defenceless, but with a feeling for jokes and a liking for dares. A man would say: I'll eat eight yards of sausages, three chickens and a candle. Yes, including the candle. Like a circus. Then he would do it, and straight after it they would carry him off on a motor-bike, purple in the face, with sightless eyes; everyone laughing at this terrible thing, death from gluttony.

One man was a sailor, always roaming the world and occasionally sending postcards to his friends in Raoul's cafe: 'Passing Parrots' Island, remembering you all.'

And there are rhythms in that countryside, sweetnesses that may have come in from the sea. I remember a child's voice one summer afternoon in a shadowy alley: 'What's the time?' 'It must be nearly four . . .' And the child said: 'And without the nearly?'

The women had attitudes and outbursts of an eastern sensuality. When I was at nursery school, there was a lay sister with black curls and a black apron, and a face red with spots that burst out because of disorders in the blood. Hard to say what her age was. Certainly her femininity was explosive, as they say. Well, she used to hug me and stroke me, all in a smell of potato peel, the stink of rancid soup and nuns' habits.

I went to a nursery school run by the nuns of San Vincenzo, who wore those big head-dresses. One day, I was put into line for a procession, and given a candle. One of the nuns, who wore glasses and looked like Harold Lloyd, gave it to me in a bossy sort of way and said: 'Don't let it blow out, Jesus wouldn't like it.' It was very windy. Being a child, I was overwhelmed by this great responsibility.

12

There was a wind and the candle mustn't blow out. What would Jesus do to me? Meantime the procession had started off slowly, trudging ahead to the sound of an accordion. A few steps, then a pause, then ahead again, then a stop. Whatever were they doing at the head of the column? We had to sing in the procession, too. 'We love God, who is our Father . . .'. In the middle of that crowd of skirts and monks and priests and nuns, there came a sudden blare of sound, mournful, solemn and lifeless. It was the band. It alarmed me so much I burst into tears.

In my first and second years at school I was in the same class as Carlini, with whom I had seen the hanged man on the Marecchia. The master was a terror to his pupils but suddenly became friendly on holidays, when the parents brought presents, a great heap piled up round his desk, as you see on the vigil of the Epiphany. After getting all these big presents, he made us sing 'Giovinezza, giovinezza, primavera di belleeeezza': he loved this long *'e'* in *bellezza.*

After primary school I was sent to a small boarding school run by monks at Fano. The stories about La Saraghina, the discovery of sex, the punishments dealt out to me, I have shown in *8½.*

I then went back to school in Rimini in Via al Tempio Malatestiano, a building which now houses the town library and art gallery. I thought it enormously tall, and it was always an adventure going up and down the endlessly long stairs. The headmaster, nicknamed Zeus, looked like the Fire-eater in a puppet show and had a foot as big as a Fiat 600, which he aimed at us children, giving kicks that could break your back. He would lie low; then suddenly a kick would shoot out and squash you like a cockroach.

These were the years of the Iliad. We read it and learned it by heart. Each one of us identified himself with one of Homer's characters. I was Ulysses, keeping himself a little apart and looking on from a distance. Titta, who was already stout, was Ajax, Mario Montanari was Aeneas, Luigino Dolci was Hector, 'tamer of horses', and Stacchiotti (who later committed suicide outside the church at Polenta) was 'swift Achilles'.

In the afternoons we used to go to a small square to act out the Trojan war, the fight between Greeks and Trojans. We went, in fact, to have a fight. Our books were tied together with a strap, as was then the custom, and we swung them round and hit each other about the head with them.

The Iliad was relived in class as well, and Homer's heroes took over from the faces of the class. One day we came to Homer's description of Ajax as a 'stupid lump of flesh'. Titta, who was Ajax, began to protest and to hate Homer, as if he had insulted him from the very beginning of the world.

When we got to the death of Hector, Luigino Dolci, who was Hector, had his finest hour. Poor Luigino! Dragged like a worm around the walls of Troy! 'Hector's corpse trailed after them, churning up the dust, his dark flowing locks dishevelled, and his once glorious features begrimed with filth of the battlefield. Such was the fate ordained from him by Zeus.' Luigi was dead. 'But the mother tore her hair and, throwing off the glittering head-dress, she gazed distraught after the corpse of her son.' The class was silent.

Stacchiotti, with a new suit of armour made for him by Vulcan, could put the Trojans to flight with a single cry. But he had one weak point, his heel. So four Trojans would get hold of him, take off his shoe, and stab him fiercely on the heel with their set squares.

Gradually, as we began to learn English, names from Edgar Wallace took over from Homer.

So Ajax became Tony Thomas (that was Titta, nicknamed Fatty), Aeneas was Jimmy Poltavo, the international swindler (Mario Montanani), and Ulysses became Colonel Black Dan Bondery (me).

We formed a trio of thieves. We decided, for instance, to steal a chicken from Colonel Beltramelli, a neighbour. As we had often read that Dan Bondery used an oxy-acetylene lamp, we tried to find a mechanic who would let us have one to carry out the theft. Unable to do so, we had to be content with wire-cutters, with which we broke into the colonel's chicken run and caught a fowl. Killing it was terrifying. Wringing a chicken is barbaric, like committing a crime.

In the evening we used to go to the sea, vanishing into Rimini's winter mists: lowered shutters, locked up boarding houses, a heavy silence and the sound of the sea.

In summer, to torment couples making love behind the boats, we would undress quickly and turn up naked, asking the man behind the boat: 'Excuse me, can you tell me the time?' As I was skinny and had a complex about it - I was nicknamed Gandhi - I refused to wear a bathing suit.

I lived a life apart, a lonely life in which I looked for famous models like the poet Leopardi to justify my fear of bathing suits, and my incapacity to enjoy myself like the others who went splashing into the sea (perhaps that is why I find the sea so

14

'. . . vanishing into Rimini's winter mists . . .' (*Amarcord*)

fascinating, as an element I have never conquered: the place from which come our monsters and ghosts). In any case, in order to fill the gap, I had turned to art. With Demos Bonini I had started a business: an art shop called FEBO. We drew caricatures and portraits of ladies, whom we visited at home. I signed myself Fellas and did the drawings, and Bonini coloured them.

The shop was opposite the cathedral, an inspiring building. In summer, when there were no customers, we would go into it: the marble seats were cool; the tombs, the bishops and medieval knights, kept watch in the gloom, protective and slightly sinister. There was an old stone pulpit with steps running up to it on which the dean, another violent smacker of boys, climbed up on Sundays to give the sermon.

Once, in August when the church was empty, I climbed up into the pulpit. The stone was as cold as a tomb. I looked out over the empty church from the pulpit. 'Dearly beloved . . .' I said softly. Then, a little louder: 'Dearly beloved . . .' Then, louder still, so that the church echoed to the sound of it: 'Dearly beloved . . .' When I came down from the pulpit I was seized with temptation to empty the alms box: and with Titta I tried to. He pretended to be praying while we dropped a magnet through the slot, tied to a piece of string. But none of the coins clung to the magnet; which was just as well, because I disliked the whole business.

The little church of the Paolotti, in contrast, had a small building shaped like a baptistery set apart from the main church, and every now and then old girls we nicknamed 'Whiskers' used to bring animals there to have them blessed by the monks. We called them 'Whiskers' because of the dark or golden hair which visibly covered their upper lips and soft, bristly cheeks. Outside the church, we would excitedly count how many 'Whiskers' had turned up from the number of bicycles heaped against the church wall. From a broken bicycle lamp, or a pedal that had lost its rubber tread, from certain home-made improvements bolted or riveted on or tied to the handle-bars with string, we could tell if the 'Whiskers' from Sant'Arcangelo was inside, with her red hair and silver lamé jersey, worn without a bra; or the two sisters from Santa Giustina, square-set and brazen, who were training to take part in the Giro d'Italia cycle race. The mere sight of one of these bicycles in particular made our hearts beat faster: it belonged to the old cat from San Leo, a grim, powerful gladiator of a woman with a great cloud of black hair and phosphorescent eyes like a lion that looked at you slowly, indifferently, without seeing you.

We would glance anxiously into the church which was filled with baaings, flutterings, brayings. At last the women would come out with their chickens and goats and rabbits, and get on their bicycles. That was the great moment! The sharp saddles slipped rapidly under the shiny black satin skirts, outlining, swelling, expanding, with dazzling gleams and sparkles, the biggest and finest bums in the whole of Romagna. There wasn't time to enjoy them all. Lots of them burst out all together, left, right and centre, and we couldn't swing round fast enough. We had to preserve a certain respectability, and this lost us a great deal. Luckily some of the women stayed sitting on their saddles a while, chatting among themselves, one foot on the ground and the other on the pedal, arching their backs, swaying about with great slow movements like waves out in the open sea; then, their hairy jaws set as they thrust down the pedals,

'The sharp saddles slipped rapidly under the shiny black satin skirts . . .'
(*Amarcord*)

toiling hard until they worked up speed, they shouted their good-byes and went back to the countryside, some of them singing.

The church of the Servi was an immense, very high, windowless building immediately past the Fulgor cinema. For years I had failed to realise that it was a church because the front and the entrance were hidden in a little square that was always crowded with market stalls. The parish priest was Don Baravelli, who gave religious instruction at our school. A small, strong, thickset man, completely bald, he did his best to exercise the Christian virtue of patience. In order to avoid throttling us, he would come into the class-room with his eyes shut, groping for the desk, and stay like that throughout the lesson: he refused to see us! Sometimes he also covered his face with his great peasant's hands, and lowered his head on to the desk. Only once did he open his eyes and then it was to see a big fire burning among the benches and us dancing around it like Red Indians.

The church of the Servi was dark, gloomy, freezing in winter, so that we became ill from going there. It became quite the thing to say: 'He got flu in the church of the Servi'. Another thing we said was: 'Would you spend a whole night there, for ten lire?' Bedassi, who was known as Tarzan, accepted the dare and one evening, with a couple of sausages, hid inside a confessional. Next morning at six, when the first old women were arriving in Church, a bray like that of a chilly donkey was heard. It was Badassi, sprawled in the confessional, snoring open-mouthed. When he opened his eyes, he said to the sacristan who had managed to shake him awake: 'Coffee please, Mum.'

For years Bedassi's confessional was a place of pilgrimage, which incredulous, admiring boys thought much more important than the paintings above the high altar.

The new Salesian church - to continue with the churches - was one we had seen being built. In fact, it had become an obligatory stop on our Sunday outings in the carriage. 'Let's go and see how the work's getting on at the new church,' someone would say. But as it was Sunday there would be no work being done and we would stay there looking at the silent scaffolding, the big motionless cranes, the heaps of sand, the mortar. When the church was opened there were a great many speeches, but the bells were ringing so loudly you couldn't understand a word. The senior officer in the militia, a certain L., blue-chinned even when he had just come out of the barber's, folded his arms halfway through the sermon, quite close to the priest, and, with the veins seeming to burst in his neck, started yelling rhythmically 'Stop-those-bells! Stop-those-bells!' and immediately all the fascists in the church started shouting their leader's order to the bells.

Some years later, when I was ten, I spent a whole summer with the Salesian brothers. I was half imprisoned. In the evening I was fetched away. I remember with a feeling of great gloom the wretched ditch of a yard with its two dreary goal-posts and all round it a high wall with wire netting two yards high on top. Beyond that netting we could hear the bells of the carriages, the rumbling of cars, the shouts and calls of free people walking about with ice-cream in their hands. The 'Slug', a waxen-faced youth of about twenty who may or may not already have been a priest, always wanted to come and talk to me and a friend of mine who had long, gentle, girlish eyes. He would offer us sticky sweets, and sigh, and say that we should become cleverer and better and come into one of the empty classrooms with him, because he wanted to teach us bel canto. The 'Slug' had a fine voice, it turned out, and knew by heart a number of songs I then thought boring which many years later I heard again at the Terme di Caracalla in a production of *Lucia di Lamermoor*.

At that time, in order to be in the swim, you went with your friends to Raoul's bar, the 'Friends' Bar', halfway along the Corso. Raoul was fat but very active, with a little round face, and the bar, which copied the bars in Milan at the time, was filled with artists, rebellious youngsters, and sportsmen. There was also a timid hint of political opposition. In winter, it was the meeting-place of the layabouts, the *vitelloni*. (In summer, everyone moved to the sea, to Zanarini's. An important point: there is a sharp division between the seasons at Rimini. It is a substantial change, not just a meteorological one, as in other cities. There are two quite separate Riminis.)

Once, in Raoul's bar, we had the idea of seeing the new year in in prison. Through some of the warders who were friends of ours, we would take sausage and rolls to the convicts, and eat them inside with them.

The prison of La Rocca was in those days full of drunks and petty thieves who had pinched a few bags of cement. That clumsy gloomy building has always stayed in my mind as a dark presence, when I remember Rimini. Opposite it was a dusty square, on which the circuses set themselves up: a large lop-sided piazza, where the city ended. The clown Pierino performed there with his circus, swapping insults with the prisoners, who yelled blue murder at the horsemen through the bars of their windows. One morning, at the end of the square, beyond the dust, I saw the prison door open. A man came out, said something to a guard, and hurried off; but when he reached the middle of the square he hesitated, stopped, and then walked back into prison.

The Grand Hotel, on the other hand, stood for riches, luxury, and oriental opulence. When I read descriptions in novels that did not quite raise my imagination to the heights I thought they should, I would pull out the Grand Hotel, like a scene shifter in the theatre using the same backcloth for every situation. Crimes, rape, mad nights of love, blackmail, suicide, torture, the goddess Kali: everything had to be set in the Grand Hotel.

We would roam round it like mice, trying to get a glimpse of the inside; but it was impossible. Then we would peer into the big yard behind (always well shaded by its palm trees, which reached the fifth floor), full of cars with fascinating, indecipherable number plates. An Isotta Fraschini: Titta would whistle with admiration. A Mercedes Benz: another soft whistle. A Bugatti . . . The chauffeurs, in their gleaming boots, smoked as they paced up and down, holding tiny fierce dogs on leads.

At pavement height, large gratings looked down into enormous kitchens. Down below the sweating, half-naked cooks never even glanced up; their pans sizzled, and flames roared up to the ceilings, as they do when the Devil suddenly appears in a puppet show. I remember watching one of the cooks immediately below me, a big young man who worked as a hospital orderly in winter and drove the ambulance as if it were a racing car. He was dripping with sweat, wearing nothing but his underpants, and sang 'O handsome corsair, with your fine blonde hair', as he threw a cutlet into the breadcrumbs.

In the evening, the Grand Hotel became Istanbul, Bagdad, Hollywood. On its terraces, curtained by thick rows of plants, the Ziegfeld Follies might have been taking place. We caught glimpses of barebacked women who looked marvellous to us, clasped in the arms of men in white dinner-jackets, a scented breeze brought us snatches of syncopated music, languid enough to make us feel faint. They played the theme tunes of American films: 'Sonny boy', 'I love you', 'Alone', which we had heard the previous winter at the Fulgor cinema and had then hummed for whole afternoons with Xenophon's *Anabasis* on the desk and our eyes staring into space,

'We caught glimpses of barebacked women . . . clasped in the arms of men in white dinner-jackets . . .' (*Amarcord*)

our throats dry.

Only in winter, in the damp and darkness and fog, did we manage to gain admission to the great terraces of the rain-soaked Grand Hotel. But it was like coming to a camp where everyone had left a long time ago and the fire was out.

In the darkness we could hear the roaring of the sea: the wind blew a freezing drizzle from the waves into our faces. The Grand Hotel, closed like a pyramid, up there with its cupolas and pinnacles vanishing among the banks of fog, was more foreign and forbidden and unreachable to us than ever.

To cheer us up, as we came away, Titta imitated the chimes of Big Ben; Jimmy Poltavo fired three times through his overcoat pocket, with the silencer on his gun; Titta, blaspheming, tried to find a dry place where, wounded to death, he could end his strange death-pangs in curses.

But once, once only, early one summer morning, I ran up the steps and with my head down crossed the terrace, which was dazzling with light, and went in . . . Just at first I saw nothing. It was very dark, and there was the cool, scented smell of wax polish, as there was in the cathedral on Sunday mornings. The peace and silence of an aquarium. Then gradually I saw sofas as big as boats, armchairs bigger than beds, the red strip of carpet slowly curving up the marble steps towards the gleam of coloured glass; flowers, peacocks, snakes, luxuriously interlaced, their tongues intertwined; from a dizzy height, miraculously suspended in mid-air, hung the biggest lamp in the world.

Behind a counter as richly ornamented as a Neapolitan hearse was a tall, silver-haired gentleman with flashing spectacles, dressed like an undertaker at a grand funeral. Holding his arm out, never even looking at me, he showed me the door.

Life went by slowly at the Café Commercio too, a respectable café on the corner of Piazza Cavour, frequented by professional men and the bourgeoisie, with wooden floors, chocolate at five in the afternoon, billiards and chess. The old people's café, which scared us a bit.

At the Café Commercio there was Giudizio, a backward fellow who helped the women to unload the trolley and worked like a donkey, because he was a donkey. At six in the evening, he suddenly stopped this pointless work and went for a walk along the sea-front, dressed as a clown. Among outsiders, he was seized with a sort of worldly rapture. In winter, though, he set up the billiard tables in exchange for a few cigarettes. He knew all the games. At night, he behaved as a kind of secondary watchman. He slammed a cap he had found somewhere on his head and went round the shops. Where the real nightwatchman had put a card saying 'Visited' under the shutters, he put another card saying 'Me too.'

One night we were in the café arguing interminably as usual when we heard the sound of a car in the street, the door opened and three foreigners appeared. It was rather as if, say, Hans Albers had turned up with Anita Ekberg and Marilyn Monroe. We all gazed ecstatically at the sight. The man, who was wearing a big fur coat, ordered a liqueur of some unavailable kind and accepted another kind. One of the women, the more astonishing, gazed into space. Then they went out, climbed into their fantastic car and vanished into the night. We were all still sitting there stunned when Giudizio, in the silence, said: 'Well, if she gave me 50 lire, I'd have that one!' He wanted to be paid! There's Romagna for you, even at the lowest level.

'E guàt' was typical of Romagna too. He was dark-skinned and had bloodshot eyes like the *goatti*, the black fish caught in the port only in March. He said he had fought in the Great War, but that was impossible because although he looked fifty he was in fact no more than thirty. He was a leather worker, and extremely good at his job. His workshop was a kind of cave without a door and he stayed inside it all day, talking to nobody. But when a war film was shown he went into the cinema at two and left at midnight, crazy, talking to himself. As if he had heard a voice, an order of some kind, he would suddenly be seized with madness. Then he would drop everything and quickly put on one of his uniforms (army, navy, he had all sorts and shapes and colours, together with a whole arsenal of knives, bayonets and hand-grenades, half real and half fake); pull down the shutters of his shop and, creeping like a cat along the walls of the houses, reach the piazza and jump down to the ground. Then he would lie, flattened out, his face against the paving-stones, quite motionless, chattering frantically in a low voice. 'Tognini! Bloody Tognini!' he would say, by which he meant the Germans. Then, with a bray like a donkey, he would jump to his feet and charge off to the attack through a hail of bullets, whining shells, explosions, crashes, curses and cries of 'Italy! Savoy!'

As a rule, by the time he got as far as Raoul's cafe, the applause of the *vitelloni* who awaited him, and the squirts from soda-water siphons which they aimed into his face, coincided with the end of the battle. Soaking wet, he would salute in military fashion, clicking his heels in all directions; then he would imitate the sad, distant sound of a trumpet in the silence, and do it so well, with such heart-rending sadness, that even the fiercest louts among the *vitelloni*, who a moment earlier had been flinging cream cakes into his face, became melancholy and heard him out till the end.

One morning we saw the ambulance stop outside Raoul's bar. The driver was inside, having a coffee, and told us all that had happened. A 'Tognino', one of those Germans who ride round the world on a bicycle, wearing shorts and a hat full of medals and feathers, had stopped outside 'E guàt's shop to ask the way. Without a word 'E guàt', who had never bothered anyone in his

life, chopped off the man's ear with one of his great knives. He was
now being taken to Imola, to the lunatic asylum. By jumping up
high, we managed to get a moment's look through the dusty windows
of the ambulance. On the camp bed, trussed like a sausage, with a
blue handkerchief cutting into his mouth, was 'E guàt'. His red
eyes were staring round, amazed and frightened. He kept shuttting
and opening them slowly, as chickens do in the market.

And what about Fafinon? Fafinon was an old man from San
Leo who was always near the wash-house on the outskirts of
Rimini. He was nicknamed 'Fafinon of the Drain' because when
he wanted to relieve himself he lay across the drain like a bridge.
He would stay there for whole afternoons at a time, naked from
the belly downwards, sitting in the cool water, whistling happily
at the swallows and sparrows. Sometimes birds came spiralling
down from the sky and touched down on his forehead and chest.
One day the washerwomen went to call the priest: it was a scandal
they could no longer bear. Fafinon told him that St Francis used
to talk to the sparrows. 'But he didn't sit naked in a drain like you,
you great pig,' the priest said from the bank.

Meeting Fafinon was a treat for us children. We would surround
him, pull his jacket and not let him go until he had done what we
wanted: because old Fafinon, apart from knowing the language
of birds, had another talent: he could produce an almost unlimited
succession of farts. All he had to do was poke certain parts of his
stomach with his finger-tips, concentrate a little, and then he was
ready. You could ask him for sounds of every kind, imitations of
musical instruments, or the sounds of all sorts of animals, tame or
wild. What fun it was! How we loved it! Fireworks, requested with
shouts and leaps, were the grand finale, when the old man sometimes actually surprised himself. We would fling ourselves on the
ground with laughing, our eyes full of tears: what a marvellous
man!

Not so pleasant were Gigino and Bestemmia; one was annoying,
the other grim. Gigino was very strong (I envied him) and was
always on the beach or the sea-front, wearing big jerseys and suede
jackets or else nearly naked, wearing briefs. Once he met a friend
on the sea-front, fully dressed and with a girl. 'I think', he said in
his reedy voice, 'you're overdressed!' And he flung him into the
canal.

Everyone laughed rather nervously at these degrading jokes.
Gigino would come to the cafe and stand near the billiard table.

24

He would say: 'This ball's useless! And this one's even worse!'.
Then we would leave. 'Good-night, you idiots,' he would say. 'I'm
going home to my mum.' Finally, one evening, he met his barber
with a girl and told her the man was married. The barber beat him
mercilessly, and so avenged all the young men in the town.

Bestemmia's nickname wasn't actually Bestemmia. But he swore
so much that he had been nicknamed with a swear-word. So anyone
who spoke to him had to use a swear-word, and be caught up in
his tragic chain of circumstances. He would swear in a way that
made you think: 'Now God's going to come down and send a
thunderbolt on Rimini.' His eyes were like daggers. If anyone leant
a bicycle against his, he would come into the café and say: 'I'll
make you eat the bishop's statue and all the pigeons on it.' Or:
'I'll make you eat the billiard table.' Or else: 'I'll take off your
whiskers, make you eat them, dose you till you're sick and make
you eat them again.'

He was a sinister figure. I would see people like him on the
piazza, in a sort of glorious topographical perspective. Then I
would see them at home, in some little back street. Once I saw a
poor bedroom and Bestemmia flung down on the bed wearing a
sweat-shirt full of holes.

Outside the Café Commercio Gradisca used to walk. Dressed in
black satin that flashed in a steely, glittery way, she was one of the
first to wear false eyelashes. Inside the café, everyone had his nose
to the glass. Even in winter, Gradisca looked as if she had just
stepped out of a band-box, with curls, the first permanent wave.
She was known as Gradisca (her real name was quite different)
because it seems that once, when a Prince of the blood royal had
stopped in Rimini, she had been suggested to him as a woman
who knew how to behave respectfully when the occasion demanded
it. When she was naked before the Prince, careful of what she had
been told she offered herself with the words 'Gradisca!' [May it
please you!]

When Gradisca passed by, all kinds of enormous appetites
were called into being: hunger, thirst, a longing for milk. Her
broad hips looked like railway engine wheels when they moved,
they suggested such powerful movement.

As I had become known through my art work, I made a
contract with the owner of the Fulgor cinema. This man looked
like Ronald Colman, and he knew it. He wore a raincoat, even in
summer, and a moustache, and always kept quite still, so as not

25

'Even in winter, Gradisca looked as if she had just stepped out of a band-box . . .' (*Amarcord*)

to lose the resemblance, as people do when they know they look like someone. The work I did for him - caricatures of the stars appearing in the films being shown, put up in shop windows to advertise them - was done in exchange for free entrance to the Fulgor cinema. In that warm sewer of vice, which is what the cinema then was, there was a woman who squirted a sweetish, smelly substance into the air. Below the screen were rough benches. Then a fence, just like the one in a stable, divided the cheap seats from the more expensive ones. We paid 11 soldi; behind us they paid 1 lire 10. In the dark we would try to get into the expensive seats because it was said that pretty girls were to be found there. But the woman on guard always caught us. She lurked in the shadows and peered out from behind a curtain, but the glow of the cigarette always gave her away in the darkness.

After doing the caricatures, I got myself and Titta and my

'... the owner of the Fulgor cinema ... looked like Ronald Colman ...'
(*Amarcord*)

brother in free. Once, when I had gone to the Fulgor cinema, I saw
Gradisca there alone, in the expensive seats. I climbed over the
fence, slipping past the watchdog in the tent, and stopped to look
at Gradisca, my heart thudding. The strip of light from the projec-
tor caught her luminous fair hair, and I sat down, rather overcome
by my feelings, first a long way from her, then gradually drawing
closer. She was smoking slowly, thick-lipped. When I reached the
seat next to her, I put out my hand. Her opulent thigh, up as far
as her garter, felt like mortadella tied up with string. She didn't
interfere, just went on looking at the screen, magnificent, silent.
My hand went further, up to the white, soft flesh. At this point
Gradisca turned slowly round to me and said kindly: 'What are
you looking for?' I was unable to continue.

Transported by this memory, I went looking for Gradisca many
years later in the country near Comasco. I was told she had married
a cousin who was a sailor and I wanted to see her again. In my

27

' "What are you looking for?" ' (*Amarcord*)

Jaguar I reached a wretched little village, then a muddy part of the river. A little old woman was hanging out washing in a garden. 'Excuse me,' I said, 'where does Gradisca live?' 'Who's looking for her?' the old woman asked. 'I'm an acquaintance. Can you tell me where she is?' 'I am Gradisca,' said the old woman. So this was Gradisca. She had lost every single trace of that triumphant, carnival glitter of hers. When I came to work it out, in fact, she must then have been sixty years old.

At that time we always stayed in town. We seldom went outside it. I remember the Collina delle Grazie, a place of pilgrimage with a Way of the Cross, to which can be traced the terrifying, miraculous, apocalyptic effect of religion which I later evoked in some sequences of my films.

Up on the hills there were a great many zig-zag paths. Once, for some ceremony in Lent, we had a great party on a hill: peasants, old women, smells, salami wrapped in paper, someone being sick. We went up on our knees, singing, to the last Station. Up in front of us all, Don Giovanni shouted: 'And he fell a second time.' Then came even more dramatic events, in a dark, deadly, bloody crescendo. At this point I was seized with fear. Religion always had something terrifying about it.

At that time, religion was joined by fascist faces. I believe some of them had beaten up my father, and suspected certain louts who hung about the bar in their black shirts. My father kept it a secret, though. When the conversation began to touch on certain matters I saw him exchanging glances with my mother, to avoid my knowing. My confusion increased the day I saw those louts I suspected singing in church, with the priest.

One of them, a certain S., was persuaded during the war in Africa to volunteer for Spain. One day when they took us from school to the station to see off the gym master who was going to the same war, we found S. there as well, looking very much less of a braggart than usual, with three or four weeping women around him. We sang 'Facetta nera' and the train set off.

At fascist meetings, I never had a complete uniform: I always lacked something - black shoes, grey-green shorts, the fez. This was a sort of lukewarm sabotage, to stop me looking wholly fascist: the protest of an off-beat temperament, instinctively averse to that militaristic, foreboding atmosphere and all those processions.

One day, Starace was to pass through Rimini. At the station, a train covered with flags appeared. The sun shone brightly, the band burst out, trumpets blared, and the train pulled up, puffing out plenty of white smoke. What a sight! Then, when the white smoke cleared, all that was left was Starace, a small man with a big nose, who said: 'Comrades of Rimini . . .' People went crazy, perhaps because the little man had mentioned Rimini. The trumpets blared again, and I think that was all Starace said. Then a war-wounded man was presented to him, carried up to him after being taken out of his wheel-chair. It was a man we used to see at the café, with empty trousers because he had no legs. On occasions like this the blind, the halt and the lame were brought forward, suddenly important: what a lot of them there were in those days, on balconies, in the piazzas, at the theatre.

We went to see the King at Forli, and were lined up on the station platform. As it was very hot I had got out of line to go and pinch an orange from a cart just behind us when, once again,

'. . . some of them had beaten up my father . . .' (*Amarcord*)

the trumpets rang out. I had just begun to poke the orange with the bayonet on my gun and was unable to get it back into place; the gym master swore. Then the train came in and a little old man with a small tuft of white moustache appeared. That was the King.

But we enjoyed ourselves, too. One fascinating place, in Rimini, was the cemetery. Never had I seen anywhere less gloomy. It was beyond a level-crossing, so it was preceded by the exciting sight of the train. The gates were lowered, clanking: beyond them was a whitish wall and a lot of niches, like children's houses. I discovered it when my grandfather died. We grandchildren were bundled into a carriage. In order to keep us quiet the driver pushed his whip through a hole in the closed carriage, trying to hit us. It was a great outing. We started running among the graves, and hiding. I remember the fascination of all those faces: the photographs on the tombs. That people dressed in a different way before then, I discovered at the cemetery. I saw so many names, all of which I knew: Baravelli, Benzi, Renzi, Fellini, the families of Rimini. The cemetery was always in process of being made, and so had a party air about it. The builders sang as they worked. A superb peasant woman, who looked after the flower stall, used to ride by on her bicycle in the mornings. She tied the flowers up in bunches with string, which she broke with her strong teeth. A blonde, she wore a half unbuttoned black satin dress and went barefoot.

We talked about this woman during the evening walk along the Corso: every evening, five hundred yards at a snail's pace. From Dovesi, the cake shop, to the Café Commercio. When the lights went on, the evening stroll began, full of wishes and bursts of laughter. There were two opposing streams, chasing each other. It sometimes seemed that people were going to wear away the lower parts of their bodies with this endless walking.

Beyond Piazza Cavour, one of the tram termini, lay the dark countryside. At the other end, beyond Piazza Giulio Cesare, another darkness. So the evening stroll took place, warm, tremulous and exciting, between those two zones of darkness.

The station, on the other hand, was the place for dreams of adventure. Trains. The bell announcing the train. The rails branching off between the hedges. As soon as the bell stopped ringing you could see the train where the rails intersected, quite silent: the noise came later. Once we saw a train that was completely blue, the *wagons lits* train. A blind went up, a man appeared in pyjamas.

Another time, after a strange day when we no longer knew what to say to each other, Titta, Montanari and Luigino Dolci and I had a last photograph taken at the sea, and went on a pilgrimage to our old haunts. Then they took me to the station. In the square some fellows stared at me. We had a vermouth at the station bar - we who never drank, as a rule - and then I got on the train. Montanari said: 'Now Federico's becoming international.' And Titta: 'Damned sh . . .' The whistle, a shudder through all the carriages, the train moving out, the houses, the cemetery.

I left Rimini in 1937. I went back in 1945. It looked like a sea of rubble. There was nothing left. All that came out of the ruins was the dialect, the familiar cadences, a call of 'Duilio! Severino!', those strange names.

Many of the houses I had lived in no longer existed. People

talked of the front, of the caves of San Marino where they had sheltered, and I felt slightly ashamed of having been out of the disaster. Then we went round to see what was left. The small medieval piazza, 'La Pugna', was quite unharmed; among the ruins, it looked like a Cinecittà film set designed by the architect Filippone.

I was struck by the way people were so busy, nesting in their wooden huts yet already talking of boarding-houses that must be built, and hotels, hotels, hotels: the desire to rebuild houses.

In Piazza Giulio Cesare the Nazis had hanged three local people. There were now flowers on the ground.

I remember that my reactions were childish. The sight seemed to me an outsize outrage. Where was that hotel, that house, that district, that café, that school? I felt that respect for some things ought to have stopped them. All right, all right, there was a war on: but did they have to destroy every single thing?

Then they took me to see a big plastic model in a shop window. It seemed the Americans had promised to rebuild everything at their own expense, as an act of reparation. The model, in fact, showed Rimini in the future. The people of Rimini looked at it. Then they said: 'It looks like an American city. But who wants an American city?'

Perhaps I had already blotted out Rimini for myself, before this. The war finished this off, physically. Then it seemed to me that as the situation had become irreversible, everything else must stay the same. But in the meantime I have discovered Rimini again in Rome. Rimini, in Rome, is Ostia.

Before that evening, I had never wanted to go to Ostia. I had heard it spoken of as 'the beach chosen by the Duce'. I had heard people say: 'Rome now has its sea', and for this reason I had disliked the thought of it. Among other things, when I was in Rome I had no idea even which side the sea was on.

One evening, when we already had the blackout, the buses were passing silently, in a shield of blue light; the half-light made the city seem more than ever the remote, solitary, overgrown town that it is. I was celebrating something in a piazza bar with some colleagues, and with the humorist Ruggero Maccari. We had been drinking: it looked as if the restaurant would have to throw us out. In the middle of that drunken hilarity Ruggero said: 'Come with me. We'll take a tram.'

When we got off the tram after that night journey I suddenly felt cooler air. We were in Ostia. Wide empty streets, big trees swaying in the wind: beyond a cement wall I had seen, as at Rimini, the sea. A black sea that made me long for Rimini; yet it was also a glorious, secret discovery, because I could now think: near Rome there's a place that's Rimini.

Indeed I often drive towards Ostia, even unconsciously. I made *I vitelloni* there, because it is an invented Rimini, more Rimini than the real one. It suggests Rimini in a theatrical, scenic and at the same time innocent way. It is my home, almost clean, almost without its visceral moods, without aggression or surprises. In other words it is a filmic reconstruction of the town in my memory, into which I can penetrate - how shall I put it? - as a tourist without being involved.

'There are now 1500 hotels and boarding houses, more than 200 bars, 50 dance-halls, and a beach 15 kilometres long. Half a million people come here every year, half of them foreigners and half Italian. Aeroplanes darken the sky every day, from England, Germany, France and Sweden . . .'

I returned to Rimini on account of this book. The man who gives me this information is the son of a school-friend of mine. It is the children who get together these days. 'Remember Anteo, the porter at the station? He owns a huge number of hotels, today.' 'The peasants on my land,' says Titta, 'have given up farming and set up four restaurants and hotels.' 'Have you seen the sky-scraper?' 'A chap here has set up a chain of hotels - on the hills for spring time, and up in the mountains for winter - so that his customers won't leave him, and he can keep them all the year round.'

The Rimini I now see is never-ending. Before there was miles of darkness around the town and the coast road was unused. The only thing to be seen were ghostly fascist buildings, the summer camping places. In winter, when we bicycled to Rivabella, we heard the wind whistling through the windows of these buildings, because the shutters had been carried off for firewood.

Now, there's no more darkness. Instead, there's 15 kilometres of night-clubs and illuminated signs, and this endless procession of glittering cars, a kind of milky way made of headlamps. Light everywhere: the night has vanished, it has fled into the sky and the sea. This has happened even in the country, at Covignano, where they have opened an extraordinarily luxurious night-club, the kind that isn't found even in Los Angeles or Hollywood; and there it is, just where the peasants' farmyards used to be, just where you used

33

to hear nothing but their mongrels barking. Today these places have turned into oriental gardens, with music and juke boxes and people everywhere, a whirligig of flashing images, a country of playthings, Las Vegas.

I saw hotels made of glass and copper and, beyond the windows, people dancing, people sitting on the terraces. Shops, enormous department stores lit by day and open all night, with all the clothes and fashions that have rolled that way from Carnaby Street, and pop-art objects; markets open at night with the most incredible tinned food, pre-packed risotto, with saffron; a false, happy atmosphere; and cut-throat competition: boarding-houses where, for just over a thousand lire, you could get breakfast, lunch, supper, a room and a beach hut: all for a handful of coins.

I no longer knew where I was. Wasn't the Chiesa Nuova here? And where was the Viale Tripoli? Were we still in Rimini? The feeling I had when I returned to Rimini immediately after the war came back to me. Then, I had seen a sea of ruins. Now, with the same bewilderment, I saw a sea of lights and houses.

The photographer Minghini laughed delightedly at this surprise of mine and drove quickly round to show me the aquarium, hotels finer than the Grand Hotel, the new districts. He kept saying: 'Three months ago this didn't exist and the chap's now bought some land beyond the river over there. They've planned to build four sky-scrapers on the Marecchia, linked by a concrete ring, for a garage to take 2,000 cars'. The ring round the four sky-scrapers will be like a crown, a promenade leading upwards, with trees: a drawing for Flash Gordon, a palace for the king of the Martians.

People kept going into the shops, in the middle of the night; people who had come there from every part of the world, their faces yellow, red and green in the light of the signs, to buy decorated ice-creams, fish from Spain, poorly-made pizzas; people who never slept because they had juke-boxes under the bed; a continuous roar of shouted songs and electric guitars, uninterruptedly, for the whole summer. Day enters night and night enters day, without a pause. A single long day that lasts four months, as it does at the North Pole. Minghini, his eyes gleaming with pleasure, said: 'You went to Rome, but here . . .' He was right. I felt foreign, defrauded, diminished. I was at a party that was no longer for me. At least, I no longer had the strength and greed to take part in it. And it was no use waiting for the night to continue in order to seek some small corner of my memories. The uproar never ceased. High up on

34

the top storeys of the houses, under the foliage of the trees, were lighted windows and records playing. On the quayside, where at one time it was dark and a few intertwined couples could hide behind the granite blocks, there was now music, and groups of Swedes lounged on the terraces of the fish restaurants. On the other side of the quay, where once you could see the tiny, tremu-lous light of a fishing boat, there was now a kind of great serpent of light.

At last, we went and sat on the terrace of the Civic Club of Rimini. Titta, who had come along, was oddly silent. I remembered how, before the war, Titta and I had stolen from the members' over-coats at the Dramatic Society. Once we pinched 73 lire, which allowed us to spend the whole winter eating cakes and chocolate. One evening, we had heard the owner of the overcoat saying: 'If I ever get my hands on the pair who took my 73 lire, I'll smash their balls for them'. And there we had been, only a step or two away, hiding behind the pages of a magazine.

Titta, gazing at the sea of people that populated the night, suddenly woke up. 'Tell me, Signor Fellini,' he said teasingly, 'you who've searched so far, what does all this mean?'

Immediately afterwards he went off to bed, because he had a court case in Venice in the morning. Minghini went with him.

I stayed on, alone. Only in the old town was there silence, and a little less light. As I drove slowly along I saw a man in a tee-shirt, smoking in a small café. It was my business-partner in the art shop, Demos Bonini, who now makes fine copper engravings. With him was Luigino Dolci, 'Hector, tamer of horses'. Both were holding glasses of fizzy drinks between their knees. Demos was saying something funny because Luigino was laughing, shaking his head and wiping the tears away with his fists, as he used to at school.

I continued roaming about. Two or three times I drove past my hotel, but I had no wish to go to bed. I let my thoughts wander in a peaceable, empty sort of way. I felt vaguely mortified, too: something I had already organised and filed away I now found had suddenly become gigantic, and grown without my permission, without asking my advice. Maybe I was even hurt! I felt that Rome was now more comforting, smaller, more homely and more familiar. In a word, more mine. I was seized by a comical form of jealousy, wanting to ask all these people - all these Swedes and Germans: 'What on earth do you see in it all? What on earth have you come here to do?'

At this point, two boys signalled that they wanted a lift. I opened the car door. They were very polite, courteous and tactful. One of them wore his hair in big fair curls, the other had a babyish fringe that reached his nose, a shirt made of antique-looking lace and orange velvet trousers.

As they never said a word, I was unable to guess where they came from. Stockholm? Amsterdam? Or were they English? In the end I said: 'Where are you from?' 'From Rimini,' they said. And that's the remarkable thing: they are all the same, they all have a common country.

'May we get out here?' they asked at a certain point. When I opened the door, the music which we had heard in the distance became very loud. It came from the fields, where an illuminated sign said: 'The Other World'. The two boys thanked me and went in. After a moment's hesitation I got out too and went inside myself. On one side, the place opened on to the street; on the other, it ran over a kind of large earth courtyard that ended up in the countryside, mingling its music with the smell of hay. Under a circus tent there was a night-club where thousands of youngsters were dancing.

They did not see me; they do not see us old campaigners on leave whose problems bore them. While we were busy discussing the change from neo-realism to realism and so on, these youngsters were growing up in silence, then they suddenly turned up like an army from another planet, an unexpected, mysterious army that ignored us.

I sat down at a table. Beside me, a boy was caressing a girl, kissing her, gently scratching her nose. Obviously she was his girl. Then another boy came up, a friend who sat down in his place while he went off to get some water-melon. I was amazed to see the friend caressing the girl in just the same way. When the first boy came back, he sat watching his friend kissing the girl, while he ate his water-melon. Then the friend went away, and vanished among the dancers. I turned to the boy who had stayed and, as if to ask him to explain this open betrayal, I said: 'Isn't she your girl?' 'She's not *my* girl,' he answered. 'She's a girl who likes being with me.' As he spoke his eyes were merely innocent, clear, and confident.

Maybe it was due to the din, which might have heralded the end of the world, or its beginning; or to weariness, or to my ignorance of a Rimini I had never seen before; or to the sight of thousands of young people bursting out of the fields and the roads and the sea:

36

whatever it was, at that moment I felt a new meaning of life in the air, as if everything was starting off at the beginning again.

In summer, at the Chez-Vous, we used to peer through the hedge into the night-club grounds. A woman in evening dress was enough to make us tremble. Now I saw that everyone was dancing in an intimate rhythm, a kind of trance, the boys separated from their partners, as we used to call them.

I was seized with a confused sort of emotion. Of course I was struck by the theatrical aspect of it all, the sound of the bands rising up into the sky, those mysterious tribes. While the sky was lightening towards dawn and the planes were passing across it, they were dancing with an unfamiliar sort of grace.

All this seemed to me a beautiful ending for a film. I should like such an ending to give people a feeling of hope for a better humanity. But there I was wrong again: souring it all by projecting it into the future. Whereas those youngsters ought to be seen for what they were, at that particular time. Then I felt I understood them better. But I was ashamed. What was I doing - I said to myself - thinking of using this experience in a film, like a vampire? And why was I moved? Perhaps because I sensed the presence of something I had never had in my own childhood and youth, when we were inhibited by the role of the Church and of fascism, and by our mothers and fathers, whom we venerated as if they were monuments.

I should like to be young today. The young look at things without judging them, without trying to refer them to other things. Many of them, knowing nothing, turn to Zen Buddhism, which seeks to create someone capable of living in the moment, spherically, totally.

The tendency to dominate is so profound in us that it makes us look with hatred at a symbol of freedom like these youngsters, with their bright, Renaissance-style clothes. How calm and brave they have to be, every single day, as they face the lynch-mob eyes of people who would like to see their heads cropped like those of the SS!

One afternoon, in Piazza di Spagna, some of them were listening to a guitar, sitting on the edge of a fountain, when the police came to round them up. They were not worried, they put up no resistance, and did nothing that looked bold or defiant. They let themselves be packed into trucks and sat quietly, with folded arms. As I happened to see this pretty incredible sight (I couldn't see why they should be sought out so particularly as a target, with so much that was disgraceful around us), I went up to the sergeant and said: 'Why are you arresting them?' 'We're not arresting them,' he replied contemptuously, having read my thoughts. 'We're detaining them. A very different thing!'

Once, in the Corso in Rome, a girl in a mini-skirt was going by. Four men who looked like car salesmen - the kind that even in winter get a tan from a sun-ray lamp, and so, though they may be bald, have sunburned heads - slightly plump, with their names engraved on chains round their wrists, said, indicating the girl: 'If you grab them and fling them against a wall, you'll get yourself arrested. But isn't that a provocation? What they're trying to say is: Grab me, grab me.'

But that's not the least bit true. Mini-skirts aren't a new sexual invitation, it's all a mistake. Girls wear them whose legs are skinny and, if anything, best kept hidden. That means, then, that they wear them for another reason. It is we, and we alone, who superimpose on them what we have within ourselves, which grew out of our absurdly repressive education, because we want a woman to do everything she does for some lubricious purpose, a purpose that just isn't there, and that we have simply invented.

At this point I can hear the cool clear voice of the Rimini writer Liliano Faenza scolding me. In the cafés of Rimini we argued over all this. Faenza, a strict, solitary soul, holds to the principle of reason like someone truly enlightened, and has a mind moved by active pessimism. In these arguments, he said, as far as I could follow him, that he didn't like today's young, because they were empty, and because they had abandoned themselves to a state of nature without seeking a meaning in things. And adults do not know how to show them one.

'We are not merely a species, that is, nature,' Faenza told me. 'We have to build ourselves up painfully into genus, to become history or spirit, as Gramsci (co-founder of the Italian Communist Party) said. The Italians,' he went on, 'have always considered the state and civil society to be childish rubbish. So they have been reduced to believing in nothing but the family. Now they no longer believe in that. So, what's left?' Faenza paused but did not wait for an answer. 'I'll tell you what,' he said. 'Italy's becoming the brothel of Europe, thanks to tourism - Italy land of sun etc. etc. And the Italians are all becoming hotel-owners.'

Afterwards Faenza wrote to me, because he is generous and wanted to provoke me, and so to help me. 'You say you want to communicate, desperately want to communicate with the young, with *those* young people. Very well. But you should do so in order to help them to come out of the island where they have shut themselves or where we have flung them; not in order to make people long for their world. Do you remember that girl who said things that couldn't be heard, from beyond the river, in the final sequence of *La dolce vita*? She was trying to communicate, from a healthier, cleaner world, with men as corrupt as the fish that chose the Rimini beach of Miramare in 1934 as a place of death and putrefaction. What was that girl saying?'

After what I had just experienced, of course I tried to imagine what the girl was saying, since Faenza had asked me so peremptorily.

'Life has no meaning, but we must give it one,' Chaplin said in *Limelight*, another thing quoted by Faenza in his rejection of today's young. Perfectly true. But if the meaning we have so far given it has brought us to our present state, then clearly we must give it a new one. And in order to give it a new one we must destroy the old. To delude ourselves that we can establish a judicious connection between an old way of life and a new one, a link that can in any way be called prudent or useful, is not merely the worst form of conservatism - worst because it is disguised as good sense - but is quite simply impossible. I believe that revolt is by its very nature intolerant of prudence and moderation, and yet every revolt that has taken place until now has always managed to lose, in some way, whatever was authentic in its aims. Perhaps the greatest lesson of every revolt, even if it is the least obvious, is a lesson in humility, which is the opposite of paternalism. Perhaps the pop groups and the drugs and a concept of life on the biological level are lessons in humility. To reject aberration and the mortification of feeling, in order to keep intact the false, useless dignity of an objective that has already been reached, or even overtaken, means merely to avoid the difficulty of becoming a genus rather than a species, to avoid the risk of taking a new step forward to become 'history or spirit'.

Those youngsters, I believe - I want to believe - find their strength in going straight along that other road, which is only theirs and which, even if their long hair falls out, cannot be compared with our short outbursts of student bohemianism. They really have started a new era, have made a profound break with

39

the past. Faced with one of today's youngsters, the young man of 1938 is like an accountant faced with a butterfly.

But what has all this to do with Rimini? Well, I felt it and thought it all there. The air was full not just of the loud, heart-rending voices of the bands. There were also the voices of the waiters talking in my own dialect. It was still my home town.

That morning I had a moment of fullness. And the wish to say, 'You've got to do it, you've got to succeed.' I actually wanted to say this into a microphone. But they would have answered: 'Succeed at what?', which is the right answer. Because they manage to stick together just because they are different, because they are themselves, because they have no one in charge of them.

Then, at dawn, as I droned on to myself about the new form my home town had taken on, all this unknown Rimini, this strange place that appeared to me to be Las Vegas, seemed to be trying to tell me, just as those young people were trying to tell me, that it had changed and so I had better change as well.

[1967]

Sweet beginnings

After the war I set up a caricature store for Americans called The Funny Face Shop; we made sketches and caricatures, and cut records for the soldiers - it was a kind of casino with 'segnorine', as the G.I.s called girls . . . I made a lot of money - proportionately, more than I ever have since. It was sort of a Wild West general store - rough-housing and fist fights. Those guys used to come in stinking drunk and wanting to paw the girls; now and then, for chivalry's sake, it was necessary to butt in, and then really crazy things would happen. Luckily, we were on the Via Nazionale across from the military police, who were billeted in the Palazzo delle Esposizioni, and there was always one of our boys on guard who used to cross the street and call the M.P.s. They'd come in clubbing everybody indiscriminately, and then we'd be closed up for a day or two.

One day Rossellini showed up. At the time I hardly knew him . . . 'Hello, good-bye,' and that was about it. In the crowd of drunken soldiers waiting to have their caricatures or portraits done or to play records I saw a fellow with a thin, immigrant's face wearing a little grey hat and a coat. It was Rossellini. I was drawing, doing a caricature, and he signalled that he wanted to tell me some-thing. I asked him could he wait awhile.

Then he came around the table to look at the sketch I had made, which was almost finished; a little clumsily, but trying to help out, he indicated that he liked it, said I'd got the likeness. However, I remember that it was a Chinese or Japanese I was drawing and I had

41

Aldo Fabrizi in *Roma, città aperta*

made the mistake of colouring him yellow, just like that, innocently.
Perhaps the soldier had seen me dipping my pen into the yellow ink
and was a little put out. He didn't say anything though. Later, when
I gave him the yellow sketch, this fellow began . . . and then
Rossellini intervened; he took my side and said in French, 'You
aren't yellow.' Actually he *was* yellow, yellow as a lemon, and
went away mad.

Then Rossellini asked me, since I knew Aldo Fabrizi very well,
if I could persuade him to act in a short film on the life of a priest,
a script that Alberto Consiglio had written, 'The Story of Don
Morosini'.

'Because, listen, everything I own's been sold and I haven't got
a red cent. I met a Contessa who will back a short and who has
written a treatment of Don Morosini, and I'm doing it.'

And in fact the next day he introduced me to this Contessa -
she was a huge woman - who said, 'Yes I'm making a short and an
animated cartoon - a cartoon with Giop, the painter. And if you

42

could speak to Fabrizi - see if he'll take 200,000 lire . . .'

So I went to talk to Fabrizi, who was acting in a play at the Salone Margherita. He wasn't at all interested. He said, 'What the hell do I care about Don Morosini. If they want me, they'll have to pay me a million.'

Then I went back to Rossellini. 'Listen, he wants a million.'

'No. We could make it 250,000 lire.'

Meanwhile Rossellini was trying to convince the Contessa to make two shorts. Finally he got an idea: to make one short with this script of Consiglio's and another on the high-spirited pranks the Roman kids played on the Germans during the war. I used to shoot the breeze with him about his plans, but unwillingly, because I had the shop to take care of. Our friend Amidei didn't seem to think much of the idea of two shorts.

One evening he said, 'Instead of making two shorts, why don't you try to make a feature? Put these two subjects together and let's build up the story about the priest . . .' And so in a week, working in my kitchen because it was the only warm place in the house, we got up this script, which was *Roma, città aperta* [*Rome, Open City*] - but frankly without much conviction. Afterwards I went back to Fabrizi with the script and talked him into doing it. We had to give him his price, but compared to a million for a short, a million for a feature seemed fairly modest. And thus *Roma, città aperta* was born.

Rossellini liked me very much. I remembered he used to laugh a lot and pull Amidei's leg; he would come to see me at night: 'Hey, look, Amidei and I wrote this dialogue. Just listen to this . . .' And when the picture was finished any old how, we laid off for a while. Then we had a screening for some exhibitors; it was disastrous.

When they saw this thing of ours, they realised that it had been made on a shoestring. Those were the nine months that I spent here in Rome . . . The nine months in Rome under the Germans was really something; even someone who stayed in bed with his eyes closed and ears plugged could feel the fear that never let up, day or night. But the script came out well precisely because it reflected this atmosphere. I saw the preview. I was very, very moved. I was enormously disturbed, shocked, that the preview should be a flop because of the annoyance and indifference of the audience - those idiotic distributors of MGM films.

One day when we were at the little De Capitani theatre on the Via degli Avignonesi reshooting some scenes there were electric cables coming out of the theatre and cluttering up the street; an American soldier fell over them and hit his nose on the ground. It started to bleed. He got up and because he was half drunk he wanted to punch somebody. I had been standing in the doorway and I went over to help him to his feet. His face was really covered with blood. 'Fascist,' he muttered, and let off a stream of curses. I understood him well enough from being in The Funny Face Shop; I had learned a little slang. And he followed the cables, kicking them angrily - kick kick kick kick kick - and followed them inside and found himself in front of Rossellini, who was standing in front of the camera. Then he looked at him a little blankly and said, 'Whazzat?'

I said, 'A film.'

'Hey, I'm an American producer,' he said. He introduced himself and sat down, his face still covered with blood. He said, 'What kind of a film is it?'

I gave him a brief description.

'Good. I want to see it.'

Since I had a feeling that fate must have made him stumble over our cable and follow it into the theatre, we showed him *Roma, città aperta* the next day - and the fellow bought it. 'I'll take it.' This wasn't true at all. He wasn't a producer. He was one of those advertising people. But these lies were the Italian cinema's good luck, for, trusting him completely, we gave him the film. This fellow went to America, showed the film to a real distributor - a man named Destries, and the latter took it and gave him some money. He came back to Italy, paid for the film, still making himself out to be a great producer, and said, 'I want to make another film with Rossellini with all of you, with Federico. I'm through with Hollywood.'

He gave us a lot of bushwa, the biggest lot of bushwa you ever heard, with extraordinary brazenness, and *Paisà* was born in this atmosphere of monstrous untruth. The guy was a nobody and didn't have a dime.

Then he returned to America and got some money out of Destries. In Italy we found another producer, Mario Conti, who stood in awe of this Rod Geiger, the man who had put up all the money. In the meantime the idea of *Paisà* came to us, episodes of the story. 'Who do you want? Gregory Peck, you say! I'll bring you everybody for nothing. They'll come with me.' So we made a list of names, Gregory Peck and Lana Turner among them. He took off for America and one day we got a cable saying: 'Meet me in Naples.'

So we went to Naples. We watched the huge liner dock; we saw a little fellow coming down the gangplank with six people. It was Geiger, and he said, 'Here are the new big American stars. To hell with Peck and Turner. Now these . . .'

We believed everything because we didn't know anything.

'This fellow is better than Paul Robeson,' and he introduced us to a Negro. 'This girl here - who needs Turner!' Later, a bit at a time, when we were speaking with these poor jerks who were extremely ill at ease and looked to us to be unimportant, one turned out to be a waiter, one of the girls was some kind of office worker, the Negro was a singer . . . In short, they were people he had just picked up for a few bucks, which the producer paid.

However, *Paisà* was born because at the right moment a company was found with plenty of Italian capital. Lots of times good things come out of idiocies. From a good thing can come a miracle.

Paisà was my first real contact with cinema. From this I learned that it was perhaps the medium of expression most congenial to me, that in view of my laziness, my ignorance, my curiosity about life, my inquisitiveness, my desire to see everything, to be independent, my lack of discipline and a capacity for real sacrifice, I felt that the cinema was the right form of expression for me.

And here is the real lesson I learned from Roberto: this humility before the camera and in a certain sense this extraordinary faith in things photographed - in men, in faces. Up to that time when I used to go to the legitimate theatre, when I used to write scripts, I never understood anything that was going on. It seemed to me that they were just wasting time. After all, I was only producing literature, and rather low in tone. There was always something ascetic about being alone with the paper. To see them work that way in a theatre, so disorganisedly, impolitely, without understanding who was giving the orders, annoyed me. I said I would never be able to become a director. Instead, working with Rossellini, I saw what struck me most forcibly.

Humility in one's attitude toward life, not presumption, not to say: 'I am telling my fantasies, my stories.' No: 'I'm trying to tell what I have seen.' And then immense faith in the human, the plastic material itself. What struck me most and finally made me understand was that seeing things with this love was really my profession and my trade, this communion which is created from time to time between you and a face, between you and an object.

I understood that to be a director and to make films could fill my life; I couldn't ask for anything more; it could become so rich, so fascinating, so moving - a thing that justifies you and helps you find a meaning . . .

[1962]

Miscellany I –
'I'm a liar, but an honest one'

1. **When I was ten,** I never missed an issue of 'Il Corriere dei Piccoli'. I found in it a way to masquerade. In 'Il Corriere dei Piccoli' I regularly read 'Bringing up Father' and 'Felix the Cat' and 'Boob McNutt' and 'The Katzenjammer Kids'.

When I was seventeen, I finished school, and then I started to work. I went to Florence and stayed for three months, selling cartoons and satirical sketches to 'Il 420', the only satirical magazine in Italy. But I wanted to go to Rome. My mother was a Roman. As soon as I came to Rome, I had the feeling that I was home. Now I consider Rome my private apartment. That is the secret seduction of Rome. It is not like being in a city, it is like being in an apartment.

I was very pale and romantic. My shirt was always dirty and my hair was long. I went to work as a secretary for 'Il Popolo di Roma' and opened the mail and took messages. I wrote stories, drew cartoons and sold them to 'Marc Aurelio' and other magazines.

I lived in a rented room. I moved from room to room, either because I could not pay the rent or because I got into romantic trouble with the landlady. After a couple of years of working for the magazine, I started to write for the radio. Giulietta was a radio actress, and I wrote a weekly programme about a young married couple for her. Four months after we met, we got married. Then I started trying to write scripts for movies. In the beginning, I wrote just jokes and gags for the movie scripts. Then I met Aldo Fabrizi. He was a comedian who wanted to make movies. So I wrote a story for him. A producer liked it and bought it. It was

47

L'ultima carozzella. Eventually, of course, I met Roberto Rossellini, and I started working part time on the screenplays of *Roma, città aperta* and *Paisà*.

2. One day I noticed that I was a director. I think I can remember the exact moment. It was the first day of shooting *Lo sceicco bianco*. It is a true story but every time I tell it everyone looks at me as though I'm dishing up a piece of pure fiction. In fact it was like this: one morning I found myself on a boat taking me from Fiumicino to a motor-cutter which was out at sea with the cast and crew of *Lo sceicco bianco* on board. At what was still almost crack of dawn I had said good-bye to Giulietta with that same accelerated heart-beat and that same anxiety with which one goes in to an exam. I had even gone into a church and had tried to pray. I was driving my little Fiat and, on the way to Ostia, one of the tyres burst. The cast and crew, as I said, were already on the ship, and out there in the middle of the ocean I could see my fate awaiting me. I had to shoot a particularly complicated scene between Sordi and Brunella Bovo. As I approached the motor-cutter I could see the faces of the film-crew, the lights and the props. I couldn't stop asking myself: What am I going to do? I couldn't remember the film, I couldn't remember anything. I only had a strong desire to run away. But I had hardly set foot on the ship than I was giving instructions, demanding this that and the other, looking through the camera. Without knowing anything, without being aware of any objective. In the few minutes' voyage from the harbour to the ship I had become an exacting, pedantic, self-willed director with all the faults and all the merits which I had always loathed and admired in real directors.

3. Sometimes I put up with interviews pretty well. I am even quite ready to talk; in fact I may talk rather too much. Afterwards, when I read over what I've said, it depresses me and I find it all rather stupid. Then I swear it will be the last time, but because I can never say No, I do the same thing again. I'd like to keep a note of the replies I've already given and then say to the journalists - who always ask the same questions, anyway - 'Look at reply No. 2005.'

To tell you the truth, I'm a bit sick of interviews. When I'm answering questions, I sometimes see myself as an oracle . . . or an idiot.

Alberto Sordi and Brunella Bovo in *Lo sceicco bianco*

4. I'm a liar, but an honest one. People reproach me for not always telling the same story in the same way. But this happens because I've invented the whole tale from the start and it seems boring to me and unkind to other people to repeat myself.

5. I love being alone with myself, and thinking. But I can be alone only among people. I can think only if I'm pushed and shoved, surrounded by difficulties, with questions to answer, problems to solve, wild beasts to tame. That warms me, sets me up.

I haven't always been like that. Before I started directing, the very idea of having to create in the middle of uproar seemed alarming. I felt like a writer who decided to write in the street, in the middle of a crowd: someone peers over your shoulder to see what you've written, someone else profits from a moment when you've decided to concentrate to get away with your pencil or paper, a third keeps yelling obsessively into your ear. That's the kind of thing that scared me at the start. And that's the stage I've reached today - I can't do anything unless I've got uproar all around me.

49

6. I like reading strip cartoons best, and accounts of trials, history books, essays, poetry sometimes, fiction seldom.

I hardly ever go to the cinema. Sometimes I go into one, watch part of the film and then leave.

I never listen to the radio. I never watch television. I've never been to a football match in my life.

I don't like parties. I don't like conversation. The only time I'm bored is when I'm forced to be with people I don't know well, making polite conversation.

I can never sit quietly. I've got to keep moving about. I love being in a car. That's often the way I see my friends: we drive around town together. I love seeing images appearing and disappearing from the window, while we're talking.

Every day I leave home at eight in the morning. I love wandering round Rome the whole day, when I'm not working.

7. I'm not a collector. I give away my books, or drop them, or lose them. I destroy everything I find uninteresting, and everything I find interesting too if I already know it. I like having as few things as possible at home.

8. I'm not ambitious. Not everyone will agree with me, but I maintain that I'm shy. I'm always astounded that I can be a film director. Earlier on, I used to think I couldn't possibly impose my will on others, that I couldn't dominate either them or myself. I didn't choose to become a film-maker: it was the cinema that chose me.

9. Frankly, I don't see myself as the fanatical telephone user that friends and colleagues have been calling me for years, with mischievous amusement. My work brings me into contact with a large number of people, which means I'm involved in an endless network of relationships, and so it's natural that a fair part of my day should be spent on the telephone. Like everyone else I consider and use the telephone as an indispensable, fast and practical means of communication. And yet this daily use of it hasn't yet managed to remove my astonishment at the fundamentally fantastic aspect of telephoning, that is, of communication at a distance. Apart from any hackneyed ideas about communication by telephone being the modern technical equivalent of ancient means of communication - telepathy, for instance - I want to make just a few odd, hurried remarks about it. I wonder, for instance, why it is easier to get out of an unexpected visit than to withstand the temptation to pick up the telephone when it keeps ringing? Just because the person speaking isn't physically present, communication on the telephone is more tenuous but more authentic, less real but more precise, more temporary but more spontaneous, more delicate but at the same time more intense. As a rule one pays more attention both to oneself and to the other person when talking on the telephone, one participates more. Feelings and impressions expand: good news becomes more exciting because right away it is more privately taken in. A disaster becomes unbearable, because the imagination is fully stretched.

Terror is terror in its purest form: nothing is more chilling than a threat or a damning criticism pronounced on the telephone. Even the dullest, silliest joke on the telephone loses its dullness and pointlessness and takes on a disarming charm. For my part, I think solitude filled with voices is far preferable and far more joyful than the physical presence of others, when it has no meaning or point to it.

10. I never make moral judgements, I'm not qualified to do so. I am not a censor, a priest or a politician. I dislike analysing, I am not an orator, a philosopher or a theorist. I am merely a story-teller and the cinema is my work.

I have invented myself entirely: a childhood, a personality, longings, dreams and memories, all in order to enable me to tell them.

I love movement around me. That is certainly the main reason why I make films. To me the cinema is an excuse to make things move. Some years ago I set up a production unit to make films by people who were young and unknown. A year later it went bust, but I'd had a lot of fun during that year. I loved the place, the atmosphere of it all: half like an English club, half like a convent.

11. I get lots of letters. I cannot answer everyone but I do reply quite often. Sometimes I keep up a long correspondence with a stranger, without really knowing why. As soon as I've read it I destroy every letter I get. I don't like keeping paper in my pockets, or around the house; without it, I feel lighter.

12. Once, long ago, I wanted to make a film that had been written by the director of a lunatic asylum in Italy. I spent three months in his asylum, disguised as a doctor. When I left I could no longer make the film. I had felt the danger. It is very hard to keep on this side of the fence, once you have gone near it . . .

I attract madmen irresistibly. That's how it is. Everywhere I go I meet them. They are immediately seized by an immense liking for me. And so am I, as a rule. But if it goes on for a while, the instinct of self-preservation reasserts itself and I start protecting myself, unconsciously . . . And then there are dramas, I'm loathed and detested . . . The doctors in mental hospitals often tease me 'Come along to us,' they say. 'If you do, you'll never get away!'

When I introduce rather odd characters into my films, people say I'm exaggerating, that I'm 'doing a Fellini'. But it's just the opposite: in comparison with what happens to me all the time, I feel I'm softening things, moderating reality to a remarkable degree.

What interests me about madmen is the fact that they're quite independent of all ties, that there's this distance between them and other things.

13. When I'm addressed as 'Maestro' I have a feeling that someone just behind me is being spoken to. I feel I'm being teased, and, worse still, that people are trying to get rid of me, once and for all. Your work becomes unimportant: you are a 'maestro' and no-one is ever going to mention it again.

14. For an artist, even the life of the feelings is on the surface: I don't think I am capable of deep feelings, except in order to make films. I have an easy-going nature, but in order to get an artistic result I am capable of being harsh and cruel.

15. I don't want to demonstrate anything; I want to show it. I don't think I could live without making films. If you want to say that it's a good thing to have regrets (which, incidentally, I don't think it is), then I regret not having made more films. I should like to have made every kind: documentaries, advertising films, children's films, melodramas to show in public parks . . .

I can watch things in a detached way, through the camera, for instance. I never put my eye to the camera. To hell with the objective. I've got to be in the middle of things. I must know everything about everyone, make love to everything around me. I don't like being just a tourist; I don't know how to be one. Rather, I'm a vagabond, curious about everything, entering everywhere, and all the time running the risk of being thrown out by the police.

16. I believe everything I'm told. I love hearing about amazing things. My capacity for marvelling is boundless. I am not blasé about anything. On the contrary, I am careful not to confine my imagination, or what it is capable of doing. As for tidying all that up, it's none of my business. My own private world is a muddle, constantly changing, and I am certainly no genius at thinking.

I claim the right to contradict myself. I don't want to deprive myself of the right to talk nonsense, and I ask humbly to be allowed to be wrong sometimes.

17. I hate logical plans. I have a horror of set phrases that instead of explaining reality tame it in order to use it in a way that claims to be for the general good but in fact is no use to anyone.

I don't approve of definitions or labels. Labels should go on suit-cases, nowhere else.

Myself, I should find it false and dangerous to start from some clear, well defined, complete idea and then put it into practice. I must be ignorant of what I shall be doing and I can find the resources I need only when I am plunged into obscurity and ignorance. The child is in darkness at the moment he is formed in his mother's womb.

18. I love houses in process of being built, districts being demolished, people who turn up late for appointments. My favourite condition is a temporary one. I love the feeling of peering in on my own life.

All I do is done as if I were always faced with disaster, as if an earthquake were about to take place very soon. It is a stimulating feeling. As a child, if a storm was approaching I couldn't control myself.

Whenever I do anything I have a feeling that I am running along the edge of a cliff, that I am just about to break my neck.

19. I dislike travelling, and am ill at ease on journeys. In Italy, I can manage it: curiosity is aroused, I know what there is behind all those faces, voices, places. But when I'm abroad this bores me: I no longer know what anything means, I can no longer make anything out, I feel excluded.

All the same, there is always an atmosphere of travel around me. Arrivals and departures, farewells and welcomes. I love this movement about me.

My friends are my fellow travellers.

20. I learnt the essence of comedy from comic strips. I discovered them, and the circus, in the same period of my life: the characters of comic strips are clowns.

Giulietta, my wife, has the gift for evoking a kind of waking dream quite spontaneously, as if it were taking place quite outside her own consciousness.

With her clown-like gift for mimicry, she embodies in our relationship my nostalgia for innocence.

When I was in the States with her, after *La strada*, people didn't know whether to smile at her or kiss the hem of her garment. They saw her as someone halfway between St Rita and Mickey Mouse.

21. Paris seems to me rather like a stage set. Everything has already been sung, framed, chosen, presented.

Some buildings in Paris are pretty gloomy, I find. For my film *I clowns* (which is about the death of clowns) I needed somewhere gloomy. I found the Gare d'Orsay, the entrance gate to the Parc Monceau, the Pont Alexandre III, and a corner of Rue Turbigo all suited to my purpose quite well. I see those places either empty, or else peopled by a few surly concierges.

I could never live in the Latin Quarter or the Marais - they are too picturesque. If I had to live in Paris, I should like a house on the Rond-Point in the Champs Elysées: there at least one is free from folklore.

22. Nothing is sadder than laughter; nothing more beautiful, more magnificent, more uplifting and enriching than the terror of deep despair. I believe that every man as long as he lives is a prisoner of this terrible fear within which all prosperity is condemned to founder, but which preserves even in its deepest abyss that hopeful freedom which makes it possible for him to smile in seemingly hopeless situations. That's why the intention of the real - that is, the deepest and most honest - writers of comedy is by no means only to amuse us, but wantonly to tear open our most painful scars so that we feel them all the more strongly. This applies to Shakespeare and Molière as well as to Terence and Aristophanes. On the other hand there is no true tragic poet - I'm thinking of Euripides, Goethe, Dante - who does not understand how to keep

54

'. . . her clown-like gift for mimicry . . .' (Giulietta Masina in *La strada*)

a certain ironic distance from even his most terrible sufferings.

That is why it is absurd to want to classify great creative men, to differentiate between comedians and philosophers, actors and authors, clowns and poets, painters and film-makers.

I have always taken Toulouse-Lautrec as a friend and brother, because, even before the invention of cinema by the brothers Lumière, he anticipated the attitudes and images of the film; also perhaps because he felt himself constantly drawn to the disinherited and the despised, to those who are designated as depraved by 'respectable' people. It's rather difficult to be certain whom one has been influenced by during one's career. But I do know for sure that as long as I've been alive I've been thrilled by those Toulouse-Lautrec paintings, posters and lithographs. This aristocrat abhorred the 'World of Beauty'; he was convinced that the purest and loveliest flowers thrive on waste land and rubbish heaps. He loved men and women, people who were hardened, battered, unaffected by social constraints. He despised painted ladies, because he abhorred hypocrisy and artifice more than any other vice. He was simple and open, a magnificent man in spite of his ugliness. That is why he is not dead - he lives on in all our hearts through his pictures.

23. I may not go to church. But Pope John! I loved that Papa John. Once I met Pope John. In a way. I was driving to the studio in my car. Suddenly, behind me, I heard sirens, horns blowing, the police. I did not know what it was. I stop for a traffic light. Then, right next to me, a black car draws up. In the back sits Papa John, wearing the big red hat. I will never forget how Papa John looked. The smile! The innocence of his face! Like a baby. It was like an apparition in a fairy tale. He looks at me. He looks embarrassed, as though he wants to apologise for making such a fuss of traffic. I make a sign. And he made the gesture of blessing.

Papa John's face was so transparent. As soon as it was published in the newspapers, all simple people saw immediately what he was - the essence of goodness. He has done something that will never be destroyed. He was a poet. What a beautiful man!

24. What does it mean, to be a Christian? If by Christian you mean an attitude of love towards one's neighbours, it seems to me that . . . yes, all my films turn upon this idea. There is an effort to show a world without love, characters full of selfishness, people exploiting

one another, and, in the midst of it all, there is always - and
especially in the films with Giulietta - a little creature who wants
to give love and who lives for love. Well, in this way even *La dolce
vita* can be defined. . . There's a priest who found a pretty fair
definition for it. He said: 'When the silence of God falls upon men.'
But, quite apart from anything solemn or biblical in this definition,
basically, yes, *La dolce vita* could really be seen in this light. In
fact, there is the silence of God in it, the lack of love. People keep
talking about love, but it is a dry sort of love, incapable of giving.
Even *La dolce vita*, then, is a profoundly Christian film.

25. I believe in Jesus: that he is not only the greatest person in the
history of the human race, but that he continues to live on in
anyone who sacrifices himself for his neighbour. I know little about
Catholic dogma, and I may be a heretic. My Christianity is rough
and ready. I don't go to the sacraments, but I think that prayer can
be thought of as an exercise to bring us closer and closer to the
supernatural.

**26. If I were to say that I cared nothing for success, I should be
lying.** Failure brings a feeling of solitude, and that is anything but
cheerful. All the same, if something I have done is not liked, I care
very little. What saddens me is unlimited admiration from someone
who praises me for the wrong reasons.

To be applauded every evening must be fine. That is why clowns
age well and live to a ripe old age. Daily applause is nourishing.

On the other hand, success and vanity are leprous diseases which
weaken a man and make him prematurely old. In the world of the
cinema serenity goes all too soon. Apart from Dreyer, who lived
like a monk, and Chaplin, who belonged to the circus world, most
film directors last only ten or fifteen years, twenty at the most.
Yesterday they made a marvellous film, today they are completely
played out.

27. You always need an excuse to set off on a journey. In the
same way you need an excuse to start a film. A creator always
needs excuses. Creators should almost be forced to create. It would
be a good idea to have a state organisation that would make artists
work without respite from morning till night.

28. I never go to the cinema. But if I happen to go, all that interests me is the story. I never take any notice of the camera movements, the sets, the technical side of it. I don't know the classics of the cinema (though I ought not to say all this). As a child I went to the cinema for the atmosphere: I loved the noise, the smell of children's urine, the emergency exit, and the way people went out into the street - men and women stunned by the spectacle, surprised by the cold, an atmosphere suggesting the end of the world, disaster, everything swept away.

29. All I want to do when I finish a picture is to fly away. I like life. I am bored by the intellectuals, or these people who call themselves intellectuals. They try to give an exact name to everything. 'A *good* woman.' 'A *bad* woman.' And they are not real intellectuals. In the original meaning of the word, an intellectual was someone who had intellect. But the people who now *call* themselves the intellectuals have become interested in the movies. They want to give an exact name to my thoughts. I do not believe an artist has or needs to have exact thoughts. Any talk he does outside of his work means nothing. It is a lot of stupidities. I do not want to have a fixed idea about life. The only thing I want to know is: *Why am I here? What is my life?* I am not sure of anything outside of my work. The older I become, the less I know. I do not follow a particular system of working or of living. I just live. I just do things.

Letter to a Marxist critic

Dear Massimo [Massimo Puccini, Italian writer and critic], I read
your letter with the greatest interest, just as I have read the articles
by some left-wing critics with whom you agree, and I hope you will
accept my frankness if I tell you that your criticisms, or rather
your researches, whose good faith I don't doubt, don't seem to me
very persuasive. Of course I'm not disputing the value of these
criticisms, that's not my job; I'm simply saying they haven't
persuaded me. And I think there must be something underneath
all this. I think we must be starting from different principles and
different premises which make it impossible, not for me to speak
to you, because I simply put my film on the screen, but for you
to listen and to respond. Perhaps it is the very principles you agree
with that makes me doubt the rightness and coherence of your
point of view; that is, your point of view as Marxists which, I must
admit, makes your criticisms lose some of their value if I compare
them with what is being said at present in Paris by Marxists who
have seen my film. You will reply that the French communists
can think what they like, that it is none of your business, but you
must admit that, quite apart from having a particular value of its
own, their opinion shows that your wish to offer advice and
directives from your own point of view is seriously contested, and
may be proved entirely wrong by anyone who starts from the
same viewpoint as yourselves. You must admit that it is neither
trifling nor irrelevant that a poet (and communist) like Aragon has
said that he considers *The Gold Rush, Battleship Potemkin* and

La strada the best films he has ever seen. And Jacques Doniol-Valcroze, who, as you know, is an exponent of the most orthodox left-wing culture, says, in his article about other forms of cinema, that '*La strada* sends a great breath of pure healthy air through the cinema of 1955. This is the real avant-garde'. In *Les Lettres Françaises*, Sadoul says of my film: 'Goodness, love of men, faith and hope in the truth dominate all Fellini's work. How can we believe the biased lies of those who try to deny the profound significance of this film?' This is how he ends his article: 'Time will pass over *La strada*. We shall see the film again. And we shall see what success (or lack of success) it has. In any case we shall see it again. And I shall be very surprised if this film - at first sight so unexpected or so irritating - does not impress itself upon our memory and does not become a milestone in the history of the cinema. In any case I am certain that Fellini is a great creator, one of the greatest revelations the cinema has produced since the beginning of this half century'.

Of course I should not have been so immodest as to quote these judgements if you had not quoted others which have appeared in Italy, and if you had not wanted to set up, not so much a dialogue, as a friendly discussion. Seeing you have quoted what someone else has written on the literary artifice which corrupts *La strada*, allow me to reply with quotations which at least contradict it. Here, for instance, is what Jean de Baroncelli writes in 'Le Monde': 'Fellini's art is essentially very far removed from any literary false-ness and wrong sort of pathos. His poetry is natural, his mystery has no artifice about it. If he owes much to Chaplin, it can be said that the pupil is worthy of his master. To repeat what Cayatte said in Venice: *La strada*, from this moment, is already a classic'.

And here is what Charensol writes in 'Les nouvelles littéraires': 'We are definitely in the presence of a poet who is like no-one else and in whom we should have total confidence'.

Dear Massimo, I could go on for quite some time putting the criticisms you make of me into some sort of proper perspective, as well as those you quote and sum up in your letter. But you are well aware of the relative value of the quotations you cited, just as you are aware, I am sure, of the insufficient seriousness of your interpretation of my film's popular success. I should now like to add something more personal about what you say on the human and moral problem that is the basis of this film, and which is not, I believe, what you seem to think it is.

60

'Zampanò and Gelsomina . . . would seem by nature to be the least likely
people to understand each other' (*La strada*)

According to me, *La strada* seeks to realise the experience which
a philosopher, Emmanuel Mounier, has rightly said is the most
important and the most basic in seeking to open up any social
prospect: the joint experience between man and man. I mean that
in order to learn the richness and the possibilities inherent in social
life, today, when so much is said about socialism, what is more
important than anything is for a man to learn to be, quite simply,
with another. I think this is what every society must learn, and that
if we do not solve this humble but necessary problem we may
tomorrow find ourselves facing a society externally well organised,
outwardly perfect and faultless, but in which private relationships,
relationships between man and man, are empty, indifferent,
isolated, impenetrable.

Our trouble, as modern men, is loneliness, and this begins in
the very depths of our being. No public celebration or political
symphony can hope to be rid of it. Only between man and man,
I think, can this solitude be broken, only through individual people
can a kind of message be passed, making them understand - almost
discover - the profound link between one person and the next.

61

La strada expresses something like this with the means available to the cinema. Because it tries to show the supernatural and personal communication between a man and a woman - Zampanò and Gelsomina, who would seem by nature to be the least likely people to understand each other - it has, I believe, been attacked by those who believe only in natural and political communication.

But the film also aspires to show things that are quite simply human and affective. It asks what function a woman may have in a relationship between individual people and how important feminine affectiveness (or, let us say, the poetry of woman) is in calling others to spirituality and love. The film shows a human example among the many possible examples, possibly the most unpromising case of human living together it would be possible to find, and tries to see how the greyness of this relationship slowly breaks out and flowers into an elementary, supernatural society. My ambition (perhaps my illusion) is that everyone can find similar cases to deal with in himself and around him, and that this film shows him how to do so, and above all gives him the wish to do so. If I am right, then our efforts will not have been in vain. If, in seeking to show how the essence of social will and the possibilities of social advance are born from a relationship, I used a situation that seemed so unsuitable and so abstract, so immediate, so drearily everyday, it is because I believe that if one is showing the transition from individualism to true socialism today, then, in order to be persuasive, this must be seen and analysed as a need of the heart, as the impulse of a moment, as a line of action in the humblest part of our lives. 'Society' must be born as a profound need of existence; it is here that it must mature, and from here that it must be launched. You will not be surprised (or perhaps you will be) if I quote two passages from Engels to you: 'The brutal indifference, the harsh isolation of each individual in his own private interests, appears all the more disgusting when these individuals are living close to one another in a small space'; 'The dissolution of humanity into monads, each one of which has a principle of life of its own and a particular object: the world of atoms is here carried to extremes'.

I think that this 'monadism', this loneliness deliberately provoked, permeates the very essence of our life today, and that we should throw some light upon it and the forces that work against it. When a film shows suffering in a concentrated and what I should call a microscopic image (the dimensions of history do not, after

62

all, matter in art) and, as far as it can, expresses the contrast between monologue and dialogue which is central to our life today and the source of so many of our troubles, it is dealing with a contemporary need, and examining it in depth; in other words, it is using realism in the way which seems to me most suited to the realist movement. I feel that the historical process which art must discover, support and illumine, can be seen in far less limited, and, particularly, far less technical and political terms than those in which you see it. Sometimes a film, while avoiding any precise representation of historical or political reality, can incarnate in mythic figures, speaking in a quite elementary language, the opposition between contemporary feelings, and can become very much more realistic than another film in which social and political matters are referred to much more precisely. This is why I do not believe in 'objectivity', at least in the way you people believe in it, and cannot accept your ideas of neo-realism which I feel do not fully capture, or even really impinge upon, the essence of the movement to which I have had the honour, since *Roma, città aperta*, to belong.

I should like to end with words from Pavese's diary (though I know Pavese is not in favour with you people nowadays): 'You would think that nothing existed now except ideas of violent revolution. But everything in history is revolution; even a renewal, a slow, peaceful discovery. Away, then, with the preconceived idea of moral renewal which needs (on the part of the other people, the activists) violent action. Away with this childish need for company and noise'.

[1955]

Letter to a Jesuit priest

My dear Father [Dr Charles Reinert, Swiss Jesuit and film publicist], you have asked me to write something about the spiritual concept of the world in my films.

This isn't easy to do, because I have never tried to develop a particular concept of life through my films.

All I can say is this: I am a man like so many others, living through my own experience, a man who looks at things around him humbly, respectfully, with naive curiosity, and above all with love. This love produces the tenderness and pity which I feel towards everyone I meet. I am not a pessimist and I don't want to be one, but my preference is for those who suffer most, who are the victims of evil, injustice and deceit.

I don't feel I can condemn anyone, but I should like to help everyone with my intuitive ideas and with my own experience. The people in my films are all born from these human contacts, from the voices I hear and collect within me and outside me, from a profound need to reply, without betraying their hopes.

Perhaps my spiritual world is, in fact, this instinctive wish to do good to those who know only evil, to make them catch a glimpse of hope, of the chance of a better life, and to find in everyone, even the worst intentioned, a core of goodness and love.

In developing these profoundly human and common themes, I often find myself faced with suffering and misfortunes which go far beyond what is bearable. It is then that intuition comes into being, as well as faith in the values that transcend our nature. In

'Cabiria is fragile, tender and unfortunate . . .' (Giulietta Masina in *Le notti di Cabiria*)

such cases, the great sea and the distant sky which I like to show in my films are no longer enough: beyond sea and sky, through terrible suffering, perhaps, or the relief of tears, God can be glimpsed - his love and his grace, not so much as a matter of theological faith, but as a profound need of the spirit.

Only thus, I think, is it possible to be true to those who suffer, only thus can we avoid betraying, with human distractions that offer nothing but wily promises, those who have always been beaten, exploited, cursed and made to suffer.

When, in my films, the lyrical quality of my inspiration - which is always an act of love - allows me to smile at the weeping face, to stretch out a hand to someone about to slip down and be lost, to show the way to someone who has always mistaken his, and when I manage to strip the falsehood from life's adventures, I feel I haven't betrayed anyone, and that I have done myself good, rather than other people.

My films are born not from logic but from love: they have no particular argument to press and no message which I feel I should impose upon others. *Lo sceicco bianco, I vitelloni, La strada, Il bidone,* and *Le notti di Cabiria* all have the one father. Thus, all are the same, and all are different.

Cabiria, my most recent creation, is fragile, tender and unfortunate; after all that has happened to her, and after the collapse of her naive dream of love, she still believes in love and in life. A lyrical, musical outburst, a serenade sung in the woods ends this last film of mine (which is full of tragedy), because in spite of everything Cabiria still carries in her heart a touch of grace. We must not try to discover just what is the nature of this grace; it is kinder to leave Cabiria the joy of telling us, at last, whether this grace is her discovery of God.

Dear Father, I leave my films to answer your question about the spiritual concept of my world as an artist.

[1957]

Via Veneto:
dolce vita

This is an odd way of starting an article on Via Veneto, but it is
many years since I was a journalist, and I can allow myself to dis-
regard the rules of the game. So let me say straight off that I never
go to Via Veneto. Well, hardly ever. So seldom that I simply
cannot be considered one of the regulars in this world-famous
street. I know that since *La dolce vita* my name has been insistently
linked with it and with the more or less smart night-life that goes
on there, with the lovely women and talented men who see the
small hours in at the café tables. While I was, with great difficulty,
seeking a producer for the film - in the days when I was preparing
it, that is, and before my lucky meeting with Angelo Rizzoli - I
met one possible producer who insisted on 'Via Veneto' being the
film's name. And even today a great many foreign journalists,
Americans in particular, telephone and beg me to introduce them
to the intellectual and erotic rites that find their end and their
beginning in Via Veneto. The trendiest say they are ready to spend
whatever is necessary, guarantee discretion and press me to bring
Anita Ekberg along. When I say that I can do nothing, that I don't
know the password that would allow me to penetrate the world of
Roman holidays, no-one believes me. People would believe me even
less if I were to tell the truth: and that is that in my film I invented
a non-existent Via Veneto, enlarging and altering it with poetic
licence, until it took on the dimensions of a large allegorical fresco.

The truth is that, in response to *La dolce vita*, Via Veneto has
transformed itself and has made a violent effort to come up to the

Fellini and Anita Ekberg during the shooting of *La dolce vita*

image I gave it in the film. Photographers have multiplied on every corner, muck-raking and gossip have become the order of the day, and starlets looking for publicity have started appearing there in nightdresses or riding into cafés on horseback. The film had already reached the suburban cinemas and I was still opening the morning newspapers with a certain trepidation, almost with a ridiculous feeling of remorse. What can Via Veneto have thought up last night to please those who feel nostalgic for the dolce vita, I wondered. From that time onwards, I must admit, I have felt slightly uneasy in the street. But in fact mine is a long-standing uneasiness and in order to trace its origins I have to go back to the early years of my time in Rome, lean years of *vitelloni*-style goings-on just before the war.

Rome as I knew it then was a tiny casbah of furnished rooms around the main station, with a jumbled population of frightened immigrants, prostitutes, confidence tricksters, and Chinamen selling ties. The fact that it was close to the station gave me a feeling of home, made me feel less far from Rimini. If things go wrong, a voice inside me kept saying, the train's there. I was tall and thin, I wore white canvas shoes and wandered about the sleazy pizza-bars and neon restaurants, trying not to let the holes in my trousers show. Imagine what, from a visual point of view, the airy Via Veneto became as it rose steeply from Piazza Barberini to the mosque-like cupolas of the 'Excelsior', and then on to the arches of Porta Pinciana, opening out onto greenery! To my scared provincial eyes it wasn't even Rome - it was some fairy-tale vision, Monte Carlo or Baghdad. In the screenplay for *La strada* there was a sequence I never used, which expressed this highly personal view of Via Veneto. Zampanò's motor-bike arriving from the Pincio swoops down the slope of Via Veneto, sputtering and popping; from inside, behind half-open, swaying curtains, Gelsomina looks out, wide-eyed, at the lights, the illuminated signs, the palm-trees and the cafés. Then she goes to sleep again and wakes up next morning in a dreary field, in the gipsies' Rome, with the great cupolas far in the background. In *Le notti di Cabiria* there is also a scene that shows pretty clearly my own feelings of inferiority in the face of Via Veneto. It is when Giulietta tries to rival the marvellous street-walkers outside the night-club where she meets Amadeo Nazzari.

I remember that, in the early days of my time in Rome I put my nose into a café near Porta Pinciana only once. There was an

'I was tall and thin, I wore white canvas shoes and wandered about the sleazy pizza-bars . . .' (Peter Gonzales as Fellini in *Roma*)

'. . . Giulietta tries to rival the marvellous street-walkers outside the night-club . . .' (*Le notti di Cabiria*)

entrance with a chiming bell and inside everything was silent, people talking softly, carpet on the floor. I felt I was entering an aquarium. The atmosphere struck me as restful and sleepy, and I thought how much I should enjoy being there a while, reading a book, perhaps, or writing one of the articles I was trying to get accepted by the newspapers. But the waiters looked askance at me - it was as if Charlie Chaplin had walked in: so I turned on my heel and went out to the sound of the chimes over the door, before anyone turned me out more noisily. At that time I began, from a distance, to recognise the faces of Flaiano, Patti, Pannunzio and Longanesi. I saw them walking up and down, talking animatedly outside Rosati's, and would have given anything to hear what they were saying, to know what was exciting them so much. But, as I have said, the very ground under my feet in Via Veneto seemed alarming. As soon as I could, I went back to the protective circle around the station, where I had, by then, made a good many friends.

One of these showed me how to beat Via Veneto: Rinaldo Geleng, now a very well-known illustrator, and then my colleague in the titanic task of scraping together enough to pay for a meal of pasta. We had begun, at first shyly, to go round the suburban restaurants drawing caricatures of the customers. I sketched the outline and Rinaldo coloured it in. One day we decided to attack the successful man's Rome, places where the rich used to meet, and at exactly the right time, between twelve and one, at the very heart of their fortress - at Rosati's or the Strega. At half past eleven we met outside the 'Excelsior', with grey sketch-books and wooden boxes of chalks tucked under our arms. At Rosati's there were high stools round the bar, an American touch that would have caused a sensation in Rimini, few customers, and the usual haughty-looking waiters. In the end we decided on a family, father, mother and a little girl of about eight or nine, with an air that was somehow un-Roman, as if they were just passing through. When we approached them I realised at once that they were looking at us respectfully, even uneasily and timidly. Obviously it was not the custom, wherever they came from, for people to go round cafés drawing caricatures. They thought it something that happened only in a capital city, an unusual, curious business.

'A portrait of the little girl?' we asked. They agreed, the mother completely convinced, the father rather less so. I started drawing, standing beside the table. The child never stopped fidgeting, and she had the sort of face that made it impossible to get a likeness. Rinaldo glanced at my first effort and this was enough to show me that it was no good. I tore up the page, begged the mother to keep her darling still, and started again. For five minutes I worked at it, but the result was hardly encouraging. Again I tore it up and started the portrait for the third time. 'No, no!' I heard someone shrieking at intervals, a few tables away. He wasn't talking to me: it was Leo Longanesi, fervent as ever, arguing with his admirers. Our eyes crossed a couple of times, and I thought his looked a little puzzled. 'No, no!' his little voice continued to say. Nothing doing. I confessed I had failed. Rinaldo offered to take over from me, but the father was unshakeable. A few harsh words escaped him, and were immediately softened by his wife. They had realised I was no good at drawing and this had somehow made them feel easier. In the end they invited us to sit down with them and offered us chocolate to drink and cakes. We gave up all pretence, took what we could, and the whole thing ended in an oddly homely, provincial atmosphere, as if we had acquired some relations. That evening we saw them off at the station and parted with tremendous good-byes and promises to write.

Every time I remember some episode from my bohemian days I feel oddly embarrassed. Perhaps I have talked too much about the time, perhaps I have a bad reputation: whichever it is, the fact remains that no-one believes me. A legend has grown up over the past few years which depicts me as an inveterate liar, story-teller and mystery-monger. A film buff who is writing a critical and biographical essay on me has had the idea of collecting everything that has been published about my life in Rome as an emigrant from Romagna, and then subjecting every detail of it to a cruel examination. He has written to my mother, to my brother, to Fabrizi, Sordi and Rossellini, to everyone who had known me and worked with me; and the answers he got must be seen to be believed. In the light of them (and my learned friend stuck them all reproachfully under my nose), I might never have existed. My brother Riccardo, for instance, couldn't exactly deny our relationship, but denied everything else, systematically. Fabrizi denied that I had worked with him as a writer, although it really seems to me that I did. A school friend said I ought never to have made *I vitelloni* because I had never known those young men at that age, having left Rimini when I was seventeen. And this is perhaps the only true thing said in the letters: because that was just it, I was never a layabout, a *vitellone*, myself; I knew those idle heroes of the seaside cafés from a distance and invented every single thing about them, including their name. With *La dolce vita* it was more or less the same, and it will continue to be so while I have the imagination to tell stories and direct films.

All the same, that first period of mine in Rome - about which I should have liked to make *Moraldo in città* [*Moraldo in the City*] as an ideal sequel to *I vitelloni* - really *was* full of adventures and surprising meetings. Perhaps they are not exactly the adventures and meetings I remember, altered as these are by the perspective of memory and the thousand stories about them. Talking of Via Veneto, for instance, another incident of my artistic partnership with Geleng comes to mind. This took place when, for lack of customers, we had given up caricatures, and had instead decided to decorate shop windows. In oil paint we would draw curvy girls on the glass and write notices about price reductions. With a bare-faced cheek worthy of a better cause I introduced myself to the

owner of a shoe shop at the lower end of Via Veneto, offering my
services as a decorator. The man, a small, thickset Roman, looked
at me without interest and was foolish enough to let me go ahead.
Faced with the window I had a moment's panic: I wasn't used to
drawing figures on a large scale. Geleng, who had gone off to paint
another shop window, had left me a sketch and I did my best to
stick to it. It was the figure of a girl, plump and curvy, well suited
to attract the attention of the passers-by. I asked for a ladder and
the shopkeeper, making a face, allowed me one. Then I began to
paint, while a group of curious people formed around me, and
very soon I felt things were not going quite right. The girl in the
drawing, in fact, when I came to copy her turned out enormous
and bosomy on top, while the lower part of her body was oddly
small. A little boy, who had stopped to watch my work with the
rest, began to give me advice: make it smaller there, bigger there,
look, that's not right. The shopkeeper came to the shop door,
glanced at my work and ostentatiously stared into the distance.
I was in a cold sweat. Only the shop-girl, a charming creature with
long black hair, was watching with sympathy and even enjoyment.
Determined to do at least part of the drawing over again, I asked
her for a wet rag. She brought it to me with a lovely smile, which
cheered me up for a moment; but as soon as I began to rub the rag
over the painted glass a murmur of disapproval rose from the small
crowd. Far from removing any traces of the oil painting, the water
simply spread it over the glass in a sort of huge whitish cloud. With
the shop-keeper's eyes now fixed upon me, I went on trying to
rub out my sketch, while the cloud increased enormously in size
and now covered almost the whole of the window.

'You need turps,' said the little boy behind me. I turned to the
shopkeeper and in a tiny voice asked if by any chance he had some
turps. He answered with a yell that nearly capsized the ladder: and,
seeing him so enraged, I gathered up all my things - paints and
brushes - and quite shamelessly took to my heels, caring nothing
for the comments of the crowd. I had almost reached Piazza
Barberini when I turned and saw the little man chasing me: 'Come
here!' he shouted. 'What do you want?' I said, without moving,
and even sounding quite bold. 'D'you know what you've done?'
I flung out my arms. 'D'you realise I shall have to clean up the
window?' I shrugged my shoulders. 'I wish I knew who told you
to go ahead!' I made a gesture, as if to say: 'Well, who?' The strange
dialogue was carried on at a distance, without my daring to approach

him. 'Come here!' the little man said again. I took a step or two in his direction. 'Come on, don't be frightened.' I got up to him, scared that he was going to clout me. But the poor fellow took out five lire and said: 'Here, get yourself some grub.'

For a while I steered clear of Via Veneto and its surroundings, afraid of being recognised as the painter of shop windows. Besides, my partner was not particularly successful at it either, so we decided to make a change. The 'Marc Aurelio' had accepted a few of my short articles in the meantime, and suddenly all was set fair, when the war intervened. Even the declaration of war is linked, in my mind, with a memory of Via Veneto. I had heard Mussolini's voice ('People of Italy, to arms . . .') on the wireless in the porter's room at the 'Marc Aurelio' and had been wandering about the streets on my own, worried and shaken. Rome was empty: in the whole of Via Veneto, with its trees fully in leaf since it was June, there wasn't a soul to be seen. Then a man came riding down on a bicycle towards Piazza Barberini without touching the pedals. He raised a hand from the handle-bars to greet me and shouted: 'Hey, war's been declared!'

The years went by and my feeling of inferiority about Via Veneto went away too. Throughout the war, the liberation and the post-war years, the intellectuals continued to gather at Rosati's, as if they were its guardians. The only difference now, was that one of them occasionally greeted me. And I myself was entering their circle more casually, through meetings with script writers and directors like Pinelli, Lattuada and Germi. We would often spend hours discussing the psychology of some character or the possible variants on some dramatic situation, sunk deep in the armchairs of a café; and meantime Rome was gradually changing outside, becoming the navel of a world sated with living in a new jazz age, waiting for a third world war, or for a miracle, or for the Martians. The cinema exploded, the Americans came, café society prospered, the women became marvellous, the sack dress came into fashion, and cars began to look like legendary monsters. One evening I sat enthralled for a long time, gazing at a fat man with a black moustache drinking mineral water at a table in the Café de Paris, enjoying the cool sunset with a girl like some fruitful goddess: it was the ex-king of Egypt, Farouk. I watched the photographers prowling round his table and realised that they were pushing their bulbs closer and closer to him, just to annoy. In the end Farouk leapt furiously to his feet, the table was overturned, people rushed up and the cameras flashed

more than ever.

I spent many evenings with the photographer-reporters of Via Veneto, chatting with Tazio Secchiaroli and the others, and getting them to tell me about the tricks of their trade. How they fixed on their victim, how they behaved to make him nervous. how they prepared their pieces, exactly as required, for the various papers. They had amusing tales to tell: waiting in ambush for hours, thrilling escapes, dramatic chases. One evening I actually took them all out to dinner, and I must admit they thought up all kinds of tall stories for my benefit. In the end Secchiaroli said: 'Stop inventing, you idiots, you're talking to an old hand at the game,' and I didn't know whether to take it as a compliment or an insult.

I started planning scenes and having ideas for characters based on the style of life which was now so precisely characteristic of the place. One evening I gave a lift to a blond young man wearing eye-shadow whom everyone called Chierichetta, as I was determined to discover what such a person was like. He told me he lived at Borgo San Pio, near St Peter's; and that he was very Catholic, loving only his mother and Jesus - so much so that he would have liked to wear his hair in a Jesus style. While we were wandering aimlessly around the Appia Antica district he burst out with his troubles, saying he wanted to change his life, that he could hear the voice of conscience, exactly as if there was someone inside him saying: 'Mind what you're doing.' He wanted to set up with a lawyer, a serious person, and let all the rest go, all the more so because there was going to be an apocalypse within the next few years and all the wicked would be swept away in a new deluge. He had a way of giving form to his fears which, though it never quite ceased to be grotesque, nevertheless had a sincerely religious note about it. What he said struck me profoundly.

With Flaiano, Pinelli and Brunello Rondi I checked my impressions of the material I had been gathering and went ahead in the vague direction of a film which would deal with the life of those years. And thus, through the warm summer evenings of 1958, along Via Veneto, *La dolce vita* was born, and with it all my arduous trek from producer to producer, from office to office, determined to fight for a film which, in professional circles, was said to be a failure before it had been started.

When we came to start work, Via Veneto became a problem. The city authorities allowed us to film in the street only from two till six in the morning and hedged this permission with all kinds of reservations. For the scene in which Marcello Mastroianni took Anita home, after her bathe in the Trevi Fountain, there were no difficulties. We started off in the middle of the night and managed to 'capture' a really lovely dawn, with Anita's teeth chattering with cold, Marcello worried over the punches he was to get from the athletic Lex Barker, and the photo-reporters, the *paparazzi*, jumping around the set like a lot of devils. The scene in the car between Marcello and Anouk Aimée was more complicated, because I didn't want to use any tricks in directing it. There were endless discussions with the police and in the end we got permission to film the scene in movement so long as we didn't ever stop and snarl up the traffic. Clemente Fracassi organised a line of cars that looked like a procession of the Three Wise Men. I started it in my car, driving half twisted backwards to see what was happening. Marcello and Anouk followed me in an open Cadillac. Anouk could hardly drive but the scene made it necessary for her to do so: she was pale, tense and frightened. Beside her, Mastroianni, who prides himself on being an experienced driver, was suffering horribly. They were followed by the car carrying the camera and then by the row of production cars, while little Fiats and mopeds carrying the assistants bustled about at the sides of the long column.

As the scene required several takes, we made the same trip by turning off round the blocks of buildings and reassembling the procession in Via Ludovisi. A large number of people had gathered on the pavements to watch this triumphal procession go by; a scene that was both swanky and slightly sordid, as it always is when you're filming in the midst of ordinary people. I remember particularly the face of a curious onlooker outside the 'Excelsior', a man wearing a beret, with a face of dark leather, like a saracen. This young fellow was waiting anxiously for me to pass and, knowing perfectly well that I couldn't stop without the skies falling, when I was just a yard or so away yelled one of those Roman words at me that cannot be printed in a newspaper. This happened four, five, six times: as soon as I arrived at the traffic lights the saracen would stare at me, grinning from a distance, savouring the prospect of insulting me. Then when I came close to him - bang, every time he would fling that word at me, always the same word but spoken each time with mounting enthusiasm. When I went by the seventh time I was fed up with him and would have stopped the car and got out and hit him if I hadn't been afraid of ruining a night's work. So I merely answered him in kind, using words and gestures that only my impotent fury at the time could justify. As soon as the filming was finished and the column of cars had broken up in Via Sardegna, I asked a couple of the toughest drivers to follow me and ran back to the 'Excelsior' to settle accounts. But the man who had sworn at me had vanished, melted away. Even today I have his image stamped on my mind, with his beret and everything else, and I still haven't given up hope of meeting him some day.

It was the shock of this incident that made me force the producers to let me build a reconstruction of Via Veneto. I had to film a number of scenes at café tables, among them the one in which Marcello meets his father, and it just wasn't possible to film them late at night or using hidden cameras. So Piero Gherardi, the designer, started taking measurements and built me a large slice of Via Veneto on Number 5 stage at Cinecittà. We even had a party there, inviting people from the other Via Veneto, and the illusion was perfect. All the stars of the film were at it: Anita, Anouk, Yvonne Furneaux, Luise Rainer, who was to appear in a scene we dropped later on. Their presence caused very delicate problems of precedence, which amused me a great deal at the party. Only towards the end of it, as an answer to the voices of gloom criticising the cost of it all and the time it was taking, did I say to a journalist: 'We've decided to have a party like this every three months while we're working on the film.' Angelo Rizzoli heard me and merely waved a threatening fist at me from the opposite pavement of our imaginary street.

The Via Veneto which Gherardi rebuilt was exact down to the smallest detail, but it had one thing peculiar to it: it was flat instead of sloping. As I worked on it I got so used to this perspective that my annoyance with the real Via Veneto grew even greater and now, I think, it will never disappear. When I pass the Café de Paris, I cannot help feeling that the real Via Veneto was the one on Stage 5, and that the dimensions of the rebuilt street were more accurate or at any rate more agreeable. I even feel an invisible temptation to exercise over the real street the despotic authority I had over the fake one. This is all a complicated business which I ought to talk about to someone who understands psychoanalysis.

In any case, as I said at the beginning, my relationship with Via Veneto is very vague: acquaintance rather than friendship. To me, Via Veneto is the traffic lights that stop me in the evening when I am going home. Via Veneto is the newspaper seller where I stop, usually after midnight, to buy the latest copy of the daily and weekly papers. And as I turn their pages, when there's a photograph of me, I hear the everlasting remark of the man in the kiosk: 'Well, Federi, you look awful in the papers. Do stand up straight when you see they're taking your picture. You've got a paunch on you like Fabrizi's.' Via Veneto, to me, is also the barber - until a while ago - Candidi Eliseo, by the Rossetti bookshop. A comforting, nineteenth-century place, with wooden panelling, and hair sprays, and coloured bottles with strange scents in them. The owners were a couple of little old men who had trained their assistants to be silent at work. At Candidi's there was never the usual chatter about football, or whether or not Lollo was in love with her husband. Everything was like a Swiss clinic for nervous disorders, it was an island in the pointless uproar of our lives. One sad morning I found the shutters closed and someone told me the two old men had retired.

Talking of beards and hair reminds me that in Via Veneto, again, I happened to see a very beautiful girl a few months ago, a girl so remarkably out of the ordinary that I wanted to see where she was going. It wasn't gossipy curiosity, I swear, it was just the curiosity aroused by the sight of something really remarkable. The girl walked decisively through a door, and I followed her; she went into the lift and so did I. She said to me: 'I'm going to the fourth floor'. Fine. On the fourth floor there was a door with something written on it. The girl went in and I followed her, and found myself faced with a rather pretty woman in a white blouse, sitting at a counter with telephones on it. She said: 'Just a moment', and disappeared. After a moment, while I was still trying to think what on earth had swallowed up the girl from Via Veneto, the telephonist reappeared and said: 'Please come this way'. I went into a small, darkish room, where a young doctor sat me down on an armchair, lit an infra-red lamp and started to look for something on my head. 'I am a trichologist,' he said after a while. This was how I learned a new word and started on a course to regenerate the skin on my head, with massage every morning by a troop of girls who look like exotic dancers but have orders not to talk to the customers. They only smile.

The story of the trichologist is another chapter in the mysteries of Via Veneto, which in fact are not really so mysterious. I must say, though, that in spite of my prejudices the street is very beautiful at nine in the morning, when the sky is excessively blue, the kitchen lads are flashing past on their bikes, the girls from the big clothes designers are passing, and waiters are serving coffee to the few customers who have managed to fall out of bed. There is a sort of suspended air about things, a tender atmosphere you breathe only in Rome. And it is this air, this atmosphere, that makes one say once again: coming to Rome means being reborn. This air and, of course, many other things. The 'dolce vita' is not just an ironic, satirical phrase. In fact, when I talk of Via Veneto, I must admit that it isn't so at all. And having got to this point, I can't deny that a certain complicity has arisen between me and the street these last few years. An indefinable feeling that isn't intimacy or love but that comes from having lived close together, a kind of long-standing familiarity that allows us to speak through hints and winks: that allows us, if you like, not to irritate each other. The traffic wardens and sometimes even the police greet me with special deference, as if I were a kind of local sheriff. Last week, a new policeman who was fining me on the spot was attacked by one of the traffic wardens. 'What do you think you're doing? You must be joking! Don't you know this is the director of *La dolce vita*?' I was so embarrassed that I had to insist on paying the fine.

This traffic warden is an odd man, crazy about the cinema and about Via Veneto. Every time he sees me he asks hopefully: 'When are we going to make another film in Via Veneto?' and I always say: 'Soon, quite soon.' At the moment I'm uneasy at having to confess that Via Veneto doesn't come into my next film. I know very little about this film myself, it is still in its embryonic stage, and sometimes I have a feeling I'm an astronaut shot out into space. It hasn't even got a name yet, but Mastroianni's wanderings won't take him to Via Veneto. After *La dolce vita*, that's a finished chapter.

[1962]

Notes on censorship

Censorship is a way of admitting our own weakness and intellectual insufficiency.

Censorship is always a political tool: certainly not an intellectual one. Criticism is an intellectual tool: it presupposes a knowledge of what it judges and opposes.

Criticism does not destroy; it puts an object in its proper place among other objects.

To censor is to destroy, or at least to oppose the process of reality.

Censorship buries away the subjects it wants to bury and prevents them, indefinitely, from becoming reality. If four or five intellectuals get together and carefully consider these subjects, it makes no difference: they have not become real to the general public, and therefore they lack true reality.

Censorship cannot be justified even as an expression of the will of an entire people which, believing it has critically surpassed certain positions and relationships, throws out the documents and texts of a certain culture, just as one might throw out certain books which one had read and thought silly and decadent.

Bearing in mind the fact that ideas cannot be prevented from spreading, we must examine how far we should go in preventing the sight of the erotic, the perverse, the macabre and the horrific in facts and forms and exhibits.

The banning of certain films, for their idiocy, perhaps, rather than for any carnal quality in them, is the kind of self-defence which

Fellini during the shooting of *Roma*

everyone ought to use. Of course, banning these films is not enough: we must go more deeply into the reasons for their stupidity and erotic qualities and shake up the inertia which always lies behind them.

In other words, it is not a problem of censorship, but of cleanliness and intelligence.

The problem of film censorship in Italy, as in the rest of the world, is entirely to do with the spread of ideas and it is for this reason that it is a burning, present-day problem.

We must admit, quite honestly, that the problem of film censorship could not be so important if it was just a matter of measuring the size of an actress' bikini or saying just how a show-girl ought to dance. If that were the case, then all we should have to do was see how censorship worked in each country and how it stimulated film-makers into thinking up ways of making pornographic films that did not fall within the letter of the law. Censorship of this kind should simply be intelligent, and capable of evolving, when necessary.

But the real problem of censorship is quite different. For instance the censorship of ideas is nothing more nor less than a system of violence, and it is perfectly pointless to make moral speeches about it.

Political censorship, too, has never helped anyone who used it to defend his own lack of reasoned arguments. As far as the cinema is concerned, in such a fragile, over-exposed kind of art we should not believe too firmly in the natural strength of ideas.

There is also a form of Italian censorship which has not been invented by any political party, but which is natural to the Italian way of life.

There is an Italian attitude present in all of us and reflected in censorship: this is a lack of self-criticism, a belief in the privilege of being Italian and in the quality of the blue sky above us.

Apart from this pride and euphoria, there is also an excessive degree of resignation, fear of authority and dogma, customs and formulas, all of which have made us very law-abiding and submissive.

All this leads straight to censorship.

[1958]

The bitter life –
of money

Yes, *La dolce vita* has been very successful. But I hope people will
not think it presumptuous of me if I say that happy as I am that
the film has been a success, even if it hadn't been, I would still
have got my satisfaction out of it. My passion is in the making of a
film. Afterwards, it's largely a matter that doesn't concern me.

I have this detached attitude, which I assure you is absolutely
sincere, to thank if, as I hope, I am able to resist the lure of success.
One has to be strong or just unconscious. I don't want to think
about it. Indeed it worries me that everybody has their own interpretation of *La dolce vita*. It takes away my freedom if everyone
wants me on their pedestal. However, don't think me too much of
a cynic if I add that they want me *after* I have made my films. I
had to try fifteen producers before I found one willing to make
La strada. After *Cabiria* and a second Oscar, I still had great difficulty finding a producer for *La dolce vita*.

Now I won't have to look for producers any more because I have
at last got my own film company. I have got at least that out of
La dolce vita. Many people think that this film has made me rich;
but I didn't have a percentage of the profits it is making all over
the world. And my salary went to pay back the producer who had
first backed the film but who wanted an American actor to play
Marcello [the role played by Mastroianni]!

My new company, Federiz, might be called a gift, or bonus
from Angelo Rizzoli, who put up the money for *La dolce vita.*
I have always had trouble with producers, you see. After my early

successes, they always wanted me to make the same film again. After the *Vitelloni* they wanted the *Vitellini*! They'd have paid me anything I asked. (But they hadn't the courage to let me make *I vitelloni* in the first place.) After *La strada* I had scores of offers. To make *Il bidone*, which I was then planning? No. To make *Gelsomina on a Bicycle* or anything with Gelsomina in the title. They didn't realize that in *La strada* I had already said all I wanted to say about Gelsomina. They all wanted Gelsomina. I could have earned a fortune selling her name to doll manufacturers, to sweet firms; even Walt Disney wanted to make an animated cartoon about her. I could have lived on Gelsomina for twenty years!

Why this insistence on sequels? Have they so little imagination? Of course, they wanted a sequel to *Cabiria*. Now, I ask you, what could that be? And now? Oh, yes, they'd all like a sequel to *La dolce vita*. They've even tried to make one of the typical Italian pot-boiler comedies with Toto. I have a great admiration for Toto but I don't see why I should let *La dolce vita* become a vehicle for a rubbishy parody.

Certainly *I vitelloni* was the one film which could have had a sequel in the idealistic sense. At one time, I did plan to make *Moraldo in the City*. But in the end, even that idea didn't appeal to me any more. And though some may think *La dolce vita* a sort of sequel to *Vitelloni*, in so far as it is the story of a young man from the provinces who has been in Rome for ten years, there is really no connexion between Moraldo and Marcello. The only connexion is the autobiographical vein that is in all my work.

My new offices in Rome just off the Piazza di Spagna are not intended to be just the headquarters of a production company. When we are working, be it on a film of mine or of one of the young directors that I intend to help, there will be room for the production managers and assistant directors. But all the year round, it will be a 'workshop' where my friends can gather to exchange ideas. Our conversation will not be the usual gossip of the cafés with no practical object. Our dreams will be realised; anyway let's hope so. I want to surround myself with saltimbanks, story-tellers and jesters, as in a medieval court. But there will be no despotism.

I know what it means for a young director to fight against the despotism of the producers. Maybe I survived myself because I created a fakir's wall around me. For others it is not so easy. They don't all have my fanaticism and they let themselves be browbeaten. If I had to give a definition of the policy of my company, I would

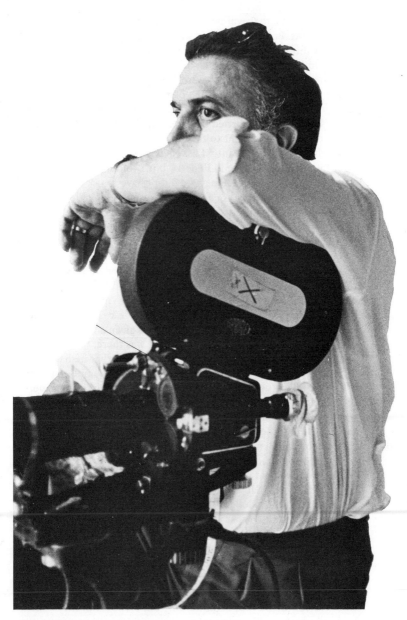

Fellini during the shooting of *Giulietta degli spiriti*

say that it is one that will never make its directors change the endings of their films. Producers always want to change the endings. I shall leave the director to do as he wishes. Rizzoli has had faith in me. I shall have faith in my directors.

Money doesn't count any more. The other day, I saw a man with a brief-case going out of the office. I asked my production manager, Clemente Fracassi, who the man was. 'Oh, he is from the bank,' he said. I was worried because usually when men from banks come to see me they want to take away my furniture or my car. 'What the devil did he want?' I asked. 'Oh, he wanted to invest eight hundred million lire in Federiz, but I told him we didn't want it,' said Fracassi. He knew he didn't have to ask me. On the Via Veneto that evening, I confessed I got quite a kick out of telling people we had refused half a million pounds!

Even in Italy, nobody quite understands how I can refuse the fabulous sums that are offered me. In the article I wrote for the last special issue of 'Films and Filming', I told you how I had turned down a quarter of a million dollars offered me by an American company to make a film about horses with an Italian star. I hear it made some people incredulous in England. Perhaps they thought it facetious of me. But, honestly, I can't take these offers seriously.

When I went to the United States, I was given a public relations man to look after me during the month I was there. When he met me at the airport, the first thing he told me was that he had 'laid on' a television interview for that evening. 'Twenty million people will be watching you,' he told me proudly. I looked in the paper and saw it was already announced that at a certain hour, somebody would be telling the American public how to cook *spaghetti alla napoletana* and the famous Italian film director Federico Fellini would show gentlemen how to kiss a lady's hand!

That poor publicity man had a terrible time with me. He just couldn't understand my attitude. He thought I was kidding or else trying to be smart. How could anyone in his senses turn down a quarter of a million dollars? I was left alone in the film producer's office to meditate on that cheque, with the contract and pen beside it. After ten minutes, when they came back and found I hadn't signed, they couldn't believe their eyes. In the end, the publicity man said, with a hurt look in his eyes, 'Maybe in Italy it's being a poet to turn down this sort of money but if you do it in the States you're a —.' He didn't know how to justify it to his boss who was convinced that I was holding out for more money. The

90

publicity man begged me to say that I was ill; that my liver troubled me; and I wanted to get back to Italy as soon as possible. The producer immediately offered me his private plane to take me to some place in Texas where he knew there was a wonderful clinic for curing liver complaints.

When I was leaving New York, the publicity man was by then resigned. I think he was even beginning to sympathise. Certainly he didn't have any more resentment. He just looked at me sorrowfully and said, 'You're a strange guy.'

I was interested in the idea of making a film about the relationship between a European and just such an American as that publicity man I had known on my previous visit. The idea appealed to me. And I had many other ideas too. But how could I make a film in America without knowing the country backwards? I wouldn't feel ready to make a film in America unless I knew what coloured tie was worn by a lawyer in Boston or how a prostitute talks in Cincinnati. Language, for me, is essential.

How do I know the difference between the speech of a Negro in the South and an emancipated Negro of the North?

How could I start shooting a scene in a New York restaurant at 4.30 in the afternoon if I have to rebuild the atmosphere in a studio? I can't depend on others.

[1961]

With '8½' in Moscow

The auditorium was huge: imagine, there were between eight and nine thousand people there. A thousand were standing. The directors of the Festival and the journalists told me that there had never been such a crowd there. I had gone there with my wife who, since *La strada* and *Cabiria*, is very well known in Russia. When Giulietta and I appeared on the stage together the applause was spontaneous and very friendly, really very encouraging because full of warmth and affection.

Then *8½* began. Russian sub-titles, few and far between, appeared now and then on the screen. Visually it was, let's say, a bit disappointing. As it was being shown in the great lecture hall of the Kremlin, every seat had a pair of earphones, and from them all came simultaneous translations in French and English . . . in other words, the whole place was crackling with metallic voices. Eight thousand pairs of earphones, however closely glued to the ears, let some sort of noise escape them: the atmosphere was that of Babel.

In spite of this the audience watched the film very attentively, almost respectfully, so much so that I felt almost uneasy. I realised suddenly that this was a personal story - my memories of childhood, my present troubles, my relationship with producers: a tale that was perhaps unsuitable for those eight thousand people of another race and with other customs. Almost, I regretted it. Just then I would have done anything to make the film different, and to reach that audience more directly.

I saw that certain points which had made the audience laugh or

Fellini during the shooting of *8½*

smile in Italy or France or America fell completely flat here - into total, cold silence. Halfway through, I had persuaded myself that the evening was going to end more or less in disaster. Then suddenly clapping broke out. And after a while more applause. During Saraghina's dance there was more applause - warm and complete - from the whole audience. And once again, before the film ended. At the very end, a final, very long period of applause, a real ovation. I really hadn't expected it.

Although the film had probably not been entirely understood, something had come across to the audience: they seemed shaken. And after it had been shown, outside in the street, people continued to clap and to call out my name for a long time.

Later in the hotel a wild-eyed young man with a long beard came up to me and almost fell on his knees to embrace me. He made a long speech in his own language. (They go in for this: quite unworried as to whether or not you understand, they carry on talking. Perhaps they are so full of feeling that they think it goes beyond words.) Then the Italian on the jury, Amidei, came up and explained that this young man was the Czech representative on the jury. And then another one came up, the Bulgarian on the jury . . . In fact, the first to congratulate me that evening were jury members from the Peoples' Republics.

But what happened later was this: the eight votes against my film, in the jury of fifteen, were cast by representatives from the Peoples' Republics. I gather Amidei turned to the Czech and said: 'But yesterday you kissed and embraced Fellini: forgive me for asking but why are you voting against him today?' With heart-rending candour the Czech representative replied: 'Yes, I really loved the film. But I've had a telegram from my government forbidding me to vote for any film that doesn't do what the Festival sets out to do . . . it's a Festival that must give prizes only to films dedicated to peace and friendship between peoples . . . etc etc.' At this point (I am repeating what I was told) Amidei asked that what the Czech member had said be put down in the minutes of the meeting. Then he broke up the discussion, supported by the American, French, Indian and Brazilian jurymen. They all came to see me at my hotel and we had a rather excited - well, a rather dramatic meeting. We even thought of getting in touch with the Italian ambassador, if only to set down what line to take in our communiqué to the press. It was, after all, soemthing of a scandal, at least on the diplomatic level. But while we were discussing it,

'During Saraghina's dance there was more applause . . .' (8½)

the Czech representative turned up again. 'There are only eight of us left,' he said to me, 'and we want to reach a solution. If we were to give you a prize, would you accept this way of putting it: "We are giving the prize to a brilliant director, an imaginative artist. What a pity, though, that his film does not contribute to peace and friendship between peoples"?' 'I might even accept,' I replied, 'if I wanted a funny story to tell for the rest of my days. But don't you see how farcical this situation is? I'm to accept a prize and at the same time a scolding. I'm to say: thanks very much, I promise not to do it again.'

The Czech, poor fellow, admitted I was right. 'Yes, yes, that's true,' he kept saying. 'Then if it's true,' I said indignantly, 'why have you come to ask me to accept a prize with those conditions attached to it?' In the end he went away, and later came back with two others (the Bulgarian and Polish representatives) to ask the dissidents to go back to work. The western members of the jury agreed and in the end they all managed to agree on a very fine formula, which didn't seem at all the result of compromise. 'We are giving the prize to *8½*, because it bears witness to the labour of an artist in search of the truth.'

And so I was given the prize. On the prize-giving evening the auditorium was even more packed than it had been for the showing of the film, and the audience applauded frantically. I was touched. All the young Russian directors, the young intellectuals and writers who had been carrying a torch for me, felt almost as if they had a prize themselves; that is, a prize which authorised them to hope and to express what they hoped.

My talks with these youngsters are possibly my most interesting memory of this Russian visit, and the thing I feel most warmly about. It was like finding old friends, but not the friends made in adult life; rather, it was like finding childhood friends, with whom one has the cosiest, naughtiest and freest relationship.

But to go back to criticism of the film: in a way it was what I expected (as I said in a radio interview as soon as I got back). I was expecting it for a very simple reason, which I will now explain. A Russian friend of mine, a film-maker with a striking resemblance to an uncle of mine from Romagna, who kept a corn-and-seed shop in Gambettola, was the most pathetic figure in the whole situation. This director (who is a big noise in the Soviet film world, as well as in politics) had seen the film before it was officially shown. He said he had been overwhelmed and bewildered by it, that there was something totally personal about it that fascinated him. Apart from this, he likes me, and his wife adores Giulietta. All the same, in spite of this almost temperamental form of liking that unites us all, as a communist and a man responsible for certain lines of thought he felt that the film might be dangerous.

Poor fellow, he was struggling between two passions: his liking for me and his belief in my freedom to express myself, and his passion for the communist ideology, which made him think the film dangerous. He tried to make me see that he couldn't give me the prize. Then one evening, after taking me on a long trip round Moscow to see the new parts of the city, the university and the hospitals, subtly trying to impress me with them, he took me to supper at his home. He was trying, in fact, to show me what point they had reached in their evolution and to make me see, without actually saying so, that a film like mine (or in any case an attitude like mine) was ahead of its time: in other words, was dangerous. Of course he didn't express himself so directly; he kept circling

96

round the subject. In the end he took me home for a meal: he is an excellent cook, and the *tortellini* he makes are another thing he has in common with the Romagna. At a certain point in the evening he said: 'I'm now going to recite some of Blok's poems to you' and went on to say something like: 'On a foggy plain lived the poets and in the morning they looked at one another with proud faces.' I said to myself: 'Here we are now: he's started playing with words like this because he's trying to tell me something.' But he went on with the poem, which was in praise of the artist as a prophetic soul able to anticipate what was coming with no obligation to current events - in other words, a seer. 'Blok wrote this poem before the Revolution,' he told me. 'After it came the Revolution and he wrote even better ones.'

He was really likeable as he tried to make me see that if my film didn't get the prize, I must understand the reason for it. And indeed, after that night trip round Moscow, and after what he had said to me, I really was persuaded that they wouldn't give me the prize and that it would be perfectly fair if they didn't. Through an interpreter, I kept saying to him: 'Don't worry, don't be upset, I understand perfectly well. Although I agree with Blok that the only way for the artist to belong to the present is for him to say what happens to him, and not to deal with current affairs or politics, I realise *8½* may worry you, I agree, don't give me the prize; it's fine as far as I'm concerned, don't get excited about it.' These words flung him into the deepest anxiety. When we got to the door of his flat (it was already dawn, five in the morning), he insisted on coming down to the main door of the building with me, and then along a wide, empty street at the end of which was the university, all lit up. He clasped my hand, to make me see, once again, that if I didn't get the prize it wouldn't be his fault, and I wrung *his* hand to show him that I didn't blame him for anything. Then, they gave me the prize after all. He sat on the stage among the cosmonauts, and applauded happily.

[1963]

Miscellany II–
'Like a puppet-master who falls in love with his puppets'

1. The cinema is very much like the circus. It is likely that if the
cinema had not existed, if I had not met Rossellini and if the circus
were still a show that had a present-day life of its own, I should
have liked to be the director of a big circus, because the circus is
just that same mixture of technique, precision and improvisation.
While the rehearsed and much-repeated show is going on, risks are
being taken - that is, life is going on too. Of course there are things
in it which have nothing to do with the creation of fantasy - the
giraffes and the tigers, all the animals. But that way of creating and
living at one and the same time, without the fixed rules which a
writer or a painter must observe, the fact of being plunged into the
action itself: that's what the circus is. It has such strength, such
bravery . . . and I feel that the cinema is exactly the same thing.
In fact, what *is* making a film? Well, it means trying to put certain
fantasies in order and telling people about them with some sort of
precision. Meanwhile, at the time the film is being made, the life
of the film unit, the meetings, the new towns which must be visited
in search of locations - the whole cinematic life - is exciting,
enriching and rewarding while the work is being done. It is a case
of finding out, at a particular moment, whether the man who is
trying to show reality to others is capable of interpreting it, because,
if he isn't, then there is no point in his starting at all.

**2. It is for this reason that my liveliest, warmest, most fervent
admiration goes to a director like Ingmar Bergman.** There's a really

gifted man, a true author, a real showman. Bergman is the living example of what I mean by showmanship, that is, he shows that all methods are permissible in art. I have seen only two of his films, *Wild Strawberries* and *The Face*. *The Face* upset me, in a way, because it is exactly the same as a story I wrote four or five years ago and meant to film - in a different atmosphere, of course. It's nordic and I'm Mediterranean, Latin, but the subject is exactly the same . . . Bergman's way of telling a story, the richness of his temperament and above all his way of expressing himself exactly as I feel a showman ought to - that is, as a mixture of magician and conjurer, prophet and clown, travelling salesman and preacher - makes him exactly what a showman ought to be.

3. Antonioni? I hope that my friendship and esteem for him will not influence me - that is, will not prevent me from giving a purely objective opinion. What I like most about Antonioni is his constancy, his consistency. He is a director who has always tried to remain faithful to his own kind of cinema, and who has imposed his own will upon it, not just because he has stood up to the demands and limitations imposed by the producers, but above all because he has kept faith with himself in a way I find truly moving. He has even managed to impose his own sort of cinema upon a public that for years refused to follow and accept him. Well, to me, that's a real lesson, an example to follow. And I think many young film-makers should be fired by his dignity and strength of character, by his faithfulness to the cinema conceived in a particular way.

4. I should love to have been making films in 1920, to have been twenty years old at the time. To have taken advantage of the pioneering days. When I started, the cinema was already an archae-ological business, it already had a history, there were already film schools and the process of intellectualising it had long ago been established. In its early days the cinema belonged to the fair-ground and I always feel a little like that about it still.

5. No film-maker has influenced me. In any case, no more and no less than the rest. The cinema as a whole has influenced me, but so, equally, have my family, my religion, my education, my marriage, my friends and so on: everything that belongs to my time, everything that has made me what I am.

I must say, all the same, that my meeting with Rossellini was a determining factor. Not as far as my way of seeing things was concerned, but because he taught me to make a film as if I were going for a picnic with friends. He made me realise that a film is a moment in life, that there is no sharp division between life and work, and that work is a form of life: not to make too many plans in advance; not to succumb to the idea that the camera is all-important; but to film life just exactly as I felt it.

Rossellini is the ancestor from whom we are all descended . . .

6. Cinéma-vérité? I prefer 'cine-mendacity'. A lie is always more interesting than the truth. Lies are the soul of showmanship and I adore shows. Fiction may have a greater truth than everyday, obvious reality. The things one shows need not be authentic. As a rule, they are better if they aren't. What must be authentic is the feeling one is trying to see and to express.

7. I had thought of making a film taken from another writer who had stirred me for a long time - that is, Dostoyevsky. And another, Dobronov. But now, to be nourished by works of art already produced by others seems somehow dangerous, and at times I think it can even be poisonous, in a way. For an artist, nourishment taken straight from life is the most important.

8. Everything that happens during its conception, or while preparations are being made for takes or cutting, is useful to a film. There really are no unimportant elements. Everything is important. There are no ideal conditions for the making of a film, or rather, conditions are always ideal, since they are what definitively allows the film to be made as it is. The illness of an actress, which makes it necessary to replace her, a refusal from the producer, an accident that holds up work - all these are not obstacles but elements in themselves, from which a film is made. What exists in the end takes over from what might have existed. It isn't just that the unexpected is part of the journey: it is, in fact, the journey itself. The only thing that matters is the inner open-mindedness of the director. Making a film doesn't mean trying to make reality fit in with preconceived ideas; it means being ready for anything that may happen.

9. When I am preparing for a film, I write very little. I prefer to draw the characters and the sets. This is something I learnt to do when I was working in provincial music-halls. From then onwards I have liked drawing the ideas that come to me, and translating every idea into an image. There are even ideas that are born all at once in the form of an image. 'Reading' it all comes later. This was particularly so with the character of Gelsomina. To me, drawing is a way of making me concentrate on the problems that arise during the preparation of a film.

10. In general, the drawings I make have only a functional purpose, and are closely linked with my work as a director. Just as the screenplay represents the literary, the verbal phase in the realisation of a film, it often happens that in the work of preparation I make sketches, designs, figures, in an attempt to fix and visually clarify a setting, a situation, a character, the costume of a certain person-age, a feeling. This casual material, these 'windbirds' (usually done on scrap-paper, backs of envelopes, etc.) serve as signposts to orientate my collaborators: the scene designer, costume artist, make-up man, etc. Unlike the screenplay, however, this work of figurative clarification is never developed systematically as some-thing indispensable. And, indeed, I make many more for some films than for others. It all depends on the nature and needs of the film on which I am working.

On the other hand, I've never thought of making drawings inspired by scenes I've already shot: to me this would seem as pointless as a dressmaker going on basting seams in a dress already perfectly finished. What I mean, you see, is that for me drawing, designing, although coming from a very natural instinct, never has an aesthetic finality. It is only an instrument, a means, a link in the chain by which fancy and imagination are anchored in a cinematic result. And even when I make doodles and drawings which serve no apparent professional necessity - a caricature of a friend seated opposite me in a restaurant, the obsessive repetition of an anatom-ical detail while waiting on the telephone, or attitudes, expressions or indecipherable graphic allusions scrawled during boring discussions - as I was saying, in these cases as well it is a matter of an exercise, a professional habit of immediately giving visual materialisation to an emotion, a snatch of some passing image, or some too pressing fancy.

11. I don't recognise, for myself, any hard and fast method of working. Though, if I had to define the way my work divides up,

I would say that at the beginning there is always a script, which largely corresponds to the structure of the film as planned.

12. In order to work, I really need to create a complete relationship and must therefore have a feeling of total friendship towards my colleagues. All of us have to have adventures together, and meetings and memories in common.

As far as my collaboration with Pinelli and Flaiano is concerned, we have managed to arrange things in such a way that we hardly ever feel we are actually working. Pinelli and Flaiano are temperamentally quite different, but they are basically complementary; that is, when they are working together, I feel that each is giving the best of himself. Pinelli is a playwright . . . probably the most serious, and the most fruitful, at present working in Italy; and Flaiano is the subtle writer, the delicate humorist, the ardent chronicler of Italian life we all know. My collaboration with them has so far been pretty happy and fertile.

As a rule, when I start getting an idea for what may be my new film (an idea which may be confused but is already insistent), I talk about it without dramatising it at all, just as if I were telling a story in a number of parts. Starting from there, we try to arrange our meetings in the least dramatic way possible. We try to meet as little as possible, and when we do meet, we behave in such a way as to avoid the heavy, formal atmosphere of a working session. We chat . . . well, we chat around the subject, and develop it . . . Then, when the story begins to have a fairly precise thread in it, we often divide up the work. Pinelli takes some scenes, Flaiano others, and I take others myself, but we do all we can to give this creation - which is the film in its very rough stage - the greatest possible freedom, that is to say, we try not to make ourselves too precise a framework, among other reasons because I shouldn't be able to work with a very carefully constructed screenplay, one that must be strictly adhered to. I need to be given freedom within an extremely elastic screenplay, not in order to improvise, exactly, but so that I can enrich a character or a situation. While the film is actually being made, the story is always enriched and given colour as it goes along. I don't think it is a good method to turn up and expect the actors to give life to a story within very strict, immovable limitations, saying to oneself this is what has been arranged in advance, and this is what must come out of it

13. Improvisation is a mirage which tricks anyone who does not know the technique needed in all creative work. Such a person thinks of inspiration as a kind of miracle, a hypnotic state that somehow settles all material problems. We ought to get rid of this legend of the inspired artist, living quite outside the world. The artist is responsible for what he does. He must use his own clear-sightedness to make something vigorous, which respects the logic of the characters, the dynamic form of the film, and its technical demands. Improvisation becomes merely a certain form of sensitivity to the demands of the particular moment; for instance, when it is a case of altering something at the last minute. In other words, it is concerned only with detail. The complete work must be carried out with mathematical precision. Making films demands a very complex degree of organisation, which implies making decisions the whole time. Hundreds of times a day decisions must be made on such things as the characters, the lighting, filming dates, the colour of so-and-so's costume, the words such-and-such is to use, the type of camera that will be suitable . . . If all this is not set down in mathematical order it is perfectly easy to see that there may never be a film. And this precision should be doubly strict when it is concerned with something that conjures up the imagination and the unknown. Having said this, it must also be said that mathematical precision does not mean a dead plan. A film is a living reality: sometimes its orders must be obeyed, sometimes one must recall it to its own internal rhythm. I don't want to make a mystery of my work, but I should like to say that my system is to have no system: I go to a story to discover what it has to tell me.

14. When this preparatory study is over, when I realise that I can go no further in that direction, I bring all this untidy material together - drawings, working notes, dialogue, photos, press-cuttings, etc - and rent an office, always in a different place and quite unknown to me, and as anonymous as possible. Then I send a small announcement to the newspapers which says, more or less: 'Federico Fellini is ready to meet all those who wish to see him.' In the next few days I see hundreds of people. Every idiot in Rome turns up to see me, including the police. It's a kind of surrealistic madhouse, which creates a very stimulating atmosphere. I look at them all very carefully, and from each visitor steal just a little of his personality. One fascinates me with a facial tic. Another interests me because of his spectacles. Sometimes I add a new

103

character to the screenplay to accommodate the new face I have discovered. I may see a thousand in order to pick two, but I assimilate them all. It's as if they were saying to me: 'Look well at us, each one of us is a piece of the mosaic you are now building up.'

15. Everything goes ahead as if, at the beginning, there were an agreement between the film that is to be born and me. As if the finished film already existed quite outside me, just as - on a very different scale - the law of gravity existed before Newton discovered it. One has to find one's way through these early stages, and rub away until one has found what produces the spark. Nothing can be hurried, things must be allowed to fall into place little by little. One must give time to attend to quite small details: the way some-one smokes, or someone else walks . . . Every detail is an opening on to a world of its own. You may see a tiny tail poking out through a hole, tug at it, and out comes an elephant.

16. The most important thing now is the choice of the faces and heads - the human landscape of the film. The fertile soil which will give the film its special character is compounded from these encounters, interviews, unconnected conversations, and from the eruption of a mass of smiles and glances. Now I no longer know whether this working method stems from my laziness or whether I am remaining superstitiously faithful to a sort of rite which is capable of bringing a film to its true fulfilment. During this time I am likely to see up to five or six thousand faces, and it is precisely these faces which suggest to me the behaviour of my characters, their personalities, and even some narrative sections of the film. I look for expressive, characterful faces for my film - faces which immediately say everything by themselves as soon as they appear on the screen.

I could if I wanted simply say to the actors in my films, be yourself and don't worry. The result is always positive. Each one of them has the face that belongs to him, that no-one else could have: and the faces always all go together, nature never makes a mistake.

17. Of course there are actors I favour for a character I have in mind; or who actually suggest a new one to me. But what matters is the face. A man may be a great actor or quite unknown, it's all the same to me. But a new face, a face I've chosen out of so many, may enrich my screenplay and completely revolutionise the film.

When I have chosen my actors, I really love them. I always make friends with them, fall in love with them: like a puppet-master who falls in love with his puppets.

18. The choice of an actor is really a critical business - weary, tiring, unpleasant. Let me give you an example. I've written and imagined that the person I want to play a certain part is, say, tall, thin, pale, distinguished-looking, well-spoken. When I look for someone to play this part, and they march past my desk - having read the newspaper announcement - all those actors and stand-ins and people, I let myself be influenced by their living, authentic reality, by the breathing humanity of their presence. As a result, if, when I'm looking for the incarnation of the character I've just described - that is, someone tall, pale, bald - I find myself faced with lots of small fat men with plenty of hair on their heads, then I'm fascinated, and I think: well . . . maybe he could play it . . . Because, you see, the man I have in mind is just a ghost, while the man in front of me is a real person, an authentic man with hairs on his fingers and a particular accent that moves me or makes me laugh, and, in the end, I come to feel that he would be suitable: that my character really could be incarnated by him. The choice then becomes extremely confusing because every living person strikes me as being more suitable than the character I have in mind.

19. Giulietta is a special case. She is not just the main actress in a number of my films, but in a very subtle way their inspiration as well. This is understandable, as she is also my lifelong companion. Giulietta, I repeat, is not the face I have chosen, but a true soul of the film. So, in the case of Giulietta's films, she herself is the theme.

With Mastroianni I have a deep sense of our working together. He's a friend, a mate of mine, someone I know well. The way Marcello really helps me is not just by being professionally good, but by abandoning himself confidently to me, which means that I can do risky things. This often happens quite naturally, without any of the sort of commitment that can be very chilling; I mean fanatical professional commitment. So, with Marcello, it's another sort of co-operation.

Sometimes I choose an actor for his face, but if, after choosing it, I find that this face doesn't suit the psychology of the man it belongs to, then I don't make the mistake of forcing him to 'get

'With Mastroianni I have a deep sense of our working together' (8½)

'Giulietta . . . is not the face I have chosen, but a true soul of the film'
(*Giulietta degli spiriti*)

inside the character'; it is the character, rather, who gets inside him.

I have no system in my work. The only system I admit to is that of not forcing things. I try to create a sort of picnic atmosphere, and in fact my actors never really know what they're going to do. Some of them won't take it, at first, because of a misunderstood sense of professional importance, or perhaps because they find themselves treated in the same way as a man I've brought in off the street. I make no difference between a star and a man brought in from the street, in the way I treat them. To me, at that particular moment, they're both vital parts of my film, and they both deserve liking and respect. In the end even the most stubborn realise that the only way to get along is to enter this romany atmosphere of companionship and daily discovery and constant moving on. Of course, I know myself where I'm trying to go; but even if we keep faith with what we have planned, we still have a wide margin in which anything may happen, at any time, to enrich the film - new encounters, say. On the other hand, you couldn't try and tell people about a journey before you'd made it. The most you could say would be that you meant to make it. But if you knew from the start what awaited you, minute by minute, then you'd never set off.

20. It's quite correct to assume a modest attitude towards life. But when one approaches the camera, this modesty must go; on the contrary, one has to be very self-assured, a tyrant, a kind of divine presence, a complete master not only of the actors but of everything.

21. The movie business is macabre. Grotesque. It is a combination of a football game and a brothel.

22. When I decide to make a film, my initial stimulus is the signing of the contract.

For people who live in the imagination there is no lack of subjects. To seek for the exact moment at which inspiration comes is false. Imagination floods us with suggestions all the time, from all directions. What we need, in order to give an exact shape to this imagination, is to find a reason - any reason - to begin; we need to connect it with physical reality. I need a brutal reason. Without this I would never give a concrete form to my ideas, I would do nothing. That's why the signature on the contract becomes a very strong reason. The weight of everyday things, physical necessities, gives a backbone to plans which, without them, would be formless. I am an artist, that is, my psychology is that of a child who must be forced to work if he is to work at all. I have to find my freedom within this obligation and these constraints.

23. No producer has ever controlled my work and I have always done what I wanted. I fight to get the sort of conditions in which I can work in peace. This is probably a result of my selfishness: if I can't do what I want, I'd sooner do nothing. Having said this, the fight itself helps me to make the film into what it is. Without it, the film would be different and, in most cases, less good.

The stupidity and mediocrity of producers have helped me; they have helped me to understand the nature of my work, to find a kind of balance without which I would have abandoned myself to idealism, to a lack of knowledge of the daily, ordinary, practical problems that are the reality of the cinema, of all art and of all things.

It would be wrong to think that the principle of production is something quite recent and concerns only the cinema. In fact, producers have always existed. Think of the conditions in which the ceiling of the Sistine Chapel was painted: 'If you don't do it I'll cut off your hands!' There, he had a very strong reason for getting on with the job! The Medici and the Borgias were producers. And the artist, at heart, finds this state of affairs suits him pretty well. He has a childish character and needs this despotic authority. Even if he mocks it, later on, in the exercise of his art.

24. Dialogue is not important to me. The function of dialogue is merely to inform. I think that in the cinema it is much better to use other elements, such as lighting, objects, and the setting in which the action takes place, since these are more expressive than pages and pages of dialogue. The sound effects should aim to emphasise the image. I work on the sound-track myself, after making the film. The noises one can get in the sound studio are very much better - quite apart from tricks and artifice - than those one can get by recording the sound live during filming. All my films have been post-synched, even the earliest. It is the Americans who insist on recording the sound during filming. Because of this, Bruno Cremer was forced to take the same scene sixty times at Cinecittà, because birds had nested in the timber-work and it took three days to find where an unwanted noise was coming from. I can't see the advantage of such a method, when you can work in conditions in the studio that are completely aseptic, as far as sound is concerned, and do what you really want to do.

I put dialogue into the film after I have made it. The actor plays better that way, not having to remember his lines. This is all the more so because I often use non-actors and, in order to make them behave naturally, I get them to talk as they would in real life. A café waiter can talk like a café waiter. I have even got people to say prayers, or make lists of numbers. Then I sort it all out in the sound studio.

25. My preference for Nino Rota as a composer comes from the fact that he seems to me to come pretty close to my themes and stories and because we work together very happily - I'm not talking of the result, just of the way we work. It isn't up to me to suggest musical ideas to him, I'm not a composer. All the same, as I've got pretty clear ideas about the film I'm making, in all its details, my work with Rota goes exactly as it does when we are elaborating the screenplay. I keep near the piano where Nino's sitting and tell him exactly what I want. Of course I don't dictate any themes to him, I can only guide him and tell him what I'm looking for. Of all composers of film music he's the humblest, I believe, because he composes extremely functional music. He hasn't got the presumption of so many composers, who want their music to be heard in the film. He knows that, in a film, music is something marginal and secondary, something that cannot occupy the foreground except in a few rare moments and, as a rule, must be content to support the rest of what is happening.

26. I love Cinecittà. I've spent the happiest part of my working life there. It's my factory, it's where I work and it's a good working tool. I'm attached to it, too, by old affections. It was a very long time ago that I first went there. At that time I was a journalist, interviewing stars and directors . . .

27. Whether modern films still need the traditional film studio is not, as it might at first sight seem, a simple problem of a technical and structural kind, but is part of the much more complex and important question of freedom of expression. Admittedly one of the most vital and authentic aspects of the cinema today is its documentary side - the way in which it bears witness to present-day reality with a socially critical attitude and a deliberate, passionately held political and ethical commitment. Obviously this kind of film has themes, and chooses subjects, that necessitate its being shot right in the middle of things, far removed from the studio. So far, so good. But if, instead of mentioning this objectively as a particular form of film-making, one goes on to say that it is the *only* valid method of film-making, and ignores or disparages every other form, then inevitably one's attitude becomes brutally repressive and discriminatory.

To me and other directors who, like me, think of the cinema as a way of interpreting and remaking reality, through fantasy and imagination, the use of the studio is an indispensable part of what we are doing. Trying to take it away from us is like trying to take the laboratory from the scientific researcher or the material he wants to turn to gold from the alchemist. In the case of a film director like myself, the studio is not merely a physical place where I work, a place that cannot be exchanged for another place or abolished altogether, but a kind of mental and psychological dwelling-place, the very means of expression for me.

As for the need to set up film studios able to cater for a modern, technically advanced form of cinema, this seems to me reasonable and productive; although I must confess that I myself, for very private reasons, like working in those old studios which are now the very opposite of functional, but which keep the haphazard, pioneering, interesting atmosphere which I find stimulating and congenial.

Finally, a couple of thoughts which this subject has suggested to me: firstly, those who want to get the cinema out of the hands of capitalism ought to try to do so not through the organic fabric of the cinema itself but through its administrators. Secondly, I wonder, rather uneasily, whether those who ask if film studios are necessary will not soon be asking whether films themselves are necessary. That would at least be a serious question.

28. I hate film festivals. They all have the kind of atmosphere I do not like - the atmosphere of a competition, which is foreign to my temperament. Festivals and New York cocktail parties: they both have the same atmosphere, with all those people who come and talk, talk, talk. And they look at me with cross eyes. When I finish a picture, if it is not released I would not care. I am glad when my pictures have success, but I would not care if they do not have success. The things I am asked to do *after* I finish a picture is the only aspect of my work that makes me tired.

Rizzoli, my producer, is a seventy-five-year-old man and he *likes* to go to film festivals. He likes to go on his yacht. He tells me, 'We will have a nice time on the yacht, we will see a lot of beautiful women, we will have good food.' I tell him, 'Film festivals are dangerous. This picture does not need publicity. Going to a film festival does not add to your prestige. Film festivals are passé.' I hate this atmosphere of examination. I hate those press conferences. But Rizzoli will do this we-have-to-defend-our-flag kind of talk, and sometimes I get so bored and tired of saying no that I might say yes. I can be very strong in everything concerning the picture, but in these other things I do not like to be unpleasant, so I might say yes. I don't like to fight with Rizzoli. And, besides, outside my work I do not have definite ideas. All I know is that I do not like this festival atmosphere of competition. When I was a boy, I always refused to put myself in competition. As a student and later on I would never compete for beautiful women. In competition I feel lost. If I put myself in the mood, I can fight, but for that I have to feel detached.

29. A film festival is something I see as an art festival. Shows of this kind should take place in a festive, even excited and stormy atmosphere, but one that is vital and open. Culture isn't necessarily dark and gloomy and intimidating, and when a cultural event consists of a show like the cinema, to decide deliberately to give this event a sad, careworn, cavernous face is flying in the face of nature. I can't see that it detracts from the show in Venice to have the authentic, central artistic part of it surrounded by a little worldliness, even a little silliness and exhibitionism. If a film is good it remains good even if part of its effect comes from a pretty woman or an actress dying for publicity, or from some picturesque character connected with it - the producer perhaps. These spicy elements may even help to get it accepted. And if a film is not much good, then it isn't automatically improved if these elements are summarily excluded.

When any cultural event becomes extremely strict and awkward in its arrangements and hysterically anxious to stick to a prearranged plan, I get the feeling that it is trying to make up for the lack of anything really good to show. In any film festival the really important thing is the films. And so, just as the whole academic and specialist paraphernalia is accepted - round-table discussions, seminars, 'meetings with the director', which nearly always turn out to be making ideological or aesthetic points in the most aggressive way - a more frivolous, worldly carnival atmosphere should be accepted too.

The selection committee should show an equal degree of liberality and impartiality. These bodies ought to base their choice on firm critical principles, but in fact they are full of prejudices and special loyalties of every kind. We live in an age that has made a cult of methodology, that makes us weakly believe that scientific or ideological ideas have the edge over reality, and that is suspicious of fantasy, of individual originality, in other words of personality. And so more and more film festivals are blackmailed by a certain sort of ideological slant into propagating a kind of culture based on collective guilt, a sense of duty, commitment and social expiation.

30. Personally I have nothing against a political cinema. If the number of films with a political and sociological background is increasing, it means that they are the result of profound, authentic demands. I disagree, however, when the political content of a film is *a priori* considered a criterion of the value of the film itself. Quite apart from the fact that added to this there has been, in recent years, an additional criterion of an economic and aesthetic kind: if a man makes a film for less than a hundred million lire on day labourers in Lucania or the Third World in order quite unjustifiably to still his own conscience, then it doesn't matter how bad it is.

I think it would be a good idea for the critics to watch films as part of a general audience. This would, I think, make their delicate task healthier, more real, and even more stimulating.

31. What is extraordinary about film critics is that they apply critical methods which are a hundred years old to work which couldn't have existed a hundred years ago.

I'm not a good critic myself. I'm a very poor witness. I put everything out of shape and I'm very partisan. I won't have any argument; discussion bores me. The critical spirit appears in me in the form of doubt. It's paralysing. For someone of my temperament, exercising the critical faculty is masochistic. Why mummify what

113

has moved you, why become lukewarm about it, why mortify it, why extinguish it? It's a physical fact: I can't bear people who try to define me too precisely.

32. As I don't consider myself exceptional, but simply a story-teller, each of my stories is really a period of my life. Deep down I feel that criticism of my work - which is the most sincere and authentic vision of myself - is unsuitable and immodest, whether it is favourable or unfavourable. Because, since I am identified totally with my work, it is as if someone were judging me as a man. I feel that my work is being judged by intruders who have no right to . . . yes, but they do have the right. But for myself, I always have the feeling that they're lacking in respect, in consideration. In the same way, I would never allow myself to criticise the human being before me: on the contrary, I try to understand him. I have a feeling that I never criticise anyone.

33. As a rule I don't like seeing films I have made. When I do, I feel indifferent. I am faced with something dead, which has lost all interest for me.

Why clowns?

The circus had broken into so many of my earlier films that it was inevitable it should occupy an entire film on its own.

How did this happen?

I had a contract with an American television company. The fact was that I had for some time been thinking of doing something for television, which is a kind of bridge between the director and his audience that is more delicate and intimate and personal than the cinema. Although I hardly ever see television programmes, the presence of this greyish eye wide open on to the house - the eye of some unearthly animal - has always fascinated me. Anyway, I wanted to have a try.

As always, what happened was not the result of any exact decision of mine.

One day, a man called Peter Goldfarb insisted that I should agree - in a very general way - to be interviewed on a programme of his called 'Experimental Hour'. This was a 55-minute programme in which people from show business and the cultural world could let themselves go and do whatever they liked. Picasso had done some sketches, with enormous success. Stravinsky had rehearsed a concert, had played and talked. Naturally none of this was true. These were projects which had yet to be realised.

Goldfarb tempted me with a number of suggestions.

'You can stay quite silent for 55 minutes. Imagine it: your eyes quite still, motionless, looking at the audience.'

'Will you pay me for that?'

'The circus had broken into so many of my earlier films . . .' (8½)

'Of course. We can even put your photograph there insted of you, if you get tired.'

I signed. Then I saw no more of Goldfarb. But the details were all set down on the contract very precisely.

While I was making *Satyricon* Goldfarb turned up again to make me keep to the contract. I suggested that he should use the rushes of *Satyricon* together with an interview. Half a day's work.

Goldfarb looked at me, half persuasive and half imperious. 'We must do something more organic,' he said.

Thus it was that I made *A Director's Notebook* - very casually, to tell the truth, as if it was just something that I had to be free of. But that sketchiness, in the right sense of the word, that haste and lightness made me feel very joyful. I felt I was walking faster, unhampered by luggage. A conversational sort of programme like that could be used with different subjects. In other words, I saw the chance of doing something new.

When the Americans made me another offer, I said yes at once. The programme had been a success with audiences in the United States; it had been put out three times, twice last year and once this year. The nature of the television medium, the intimate relationship with the audience which it allows, and, at the same time, the memory of that effortless television programme of mine, all persuaded me that I must try to bear witness to things as they were, instead of lingering over nostalgic memories or making forecasts of the future. I felt that what I ought to do was look at reality plain and simple, and not try to make the invisible visible. All my good intentions were destined to fail, however. When an artist tries to plan things from the outside, he always goes wrong.

Meantime, though, my 'white clown' had suggested to me a series of portraits that would coincide with certain large subjects of the contemporary world: Mao, an American factory, the Pope, my home town, etc. I would make them as best I could, I told myself soothingly. (I'll explain later the symbolic meaning that the 'white clown' has for me, but for the moment I will confine myself to describing it as a sort of moral yardstick like Pinocchio's talking cricket.)

The executives of the television company, though they changed continuously (I never talked to the same person twice), had accepted all these subjects with great enthusiasm. So, I began. I talked to Antonello Trombadori because I wanted to interview Mao. If I failed to interview him, then I would tell the story of my failure.

'The circus had broken into so many of my earlier films . . .' (*Giulietta degli spiriti*)

But I could not start *filming* right away. I always need a certain period of time in order to sort out my feelings and recreate them in a more precise way.

So I suggested to the new executives of the television company that we should agree on this: to make two 'specials' in the first year, one on Mao and one on a Tibetan monastery. I would set out with an organiser and a colleague. They would pay all expenses: planes, submarines, balloons: everything that might help the research, in other words. When I returned I would tell them whether or not I was in a position to undertake the work.

My precautions were due to a mixture of laziness and fear. My commitment to my work is total. I seem to give myself to it completely. Therefore work, to me, is a complete part of life. I cannot do it in a detached, professional way.

The fact was that just then I didn't think I could really take a

trip to China: just because it would be, as I was saying, not a professional matter but a choice that was part of my life. Apart from
that, it seems logical to think that my resistance was also due to
the need to apply my type of selection (which is typical of every
artistic operation) to things. And my selectivity makes me - unfor-
tunately in the circumstances - into an anti-journalist, an anti-witness.

In the end the whole thing fell through because of certain fears
on the part of the company's very latest executives, who wanted to
put a clause into the contract saying they reserved the right to
broadcast my work or not. But I cannot work under these conditions.
If I cannot be sure of talking to an audience, I cannot work.

At this point, Italian television turned up. We were to change
the subjects and deal with something Italian.

'Let's make a film about the clowns, who are the ambassadors
of my calling,' I suggested. One Sunday afternoon I chatted about
it with Bernardino Zapponi, in his house at Zagarolo. We made a
trip to Paris looking for something - I didn't know what - and when
we got back, after a few days, the screenplay was done. In other
words, things had started moving, without too much pondering over
them. I found myself saying 'the clowns'. Then I found myself
dealing with them.

The back lanes

What can I say about my relationship with television? For the
moment, the experience is worthwhile only from one point of
view: that is, for the ease and casualness with which I face it. This
particular state, I think, is favourable to the imagination, and is a
sign of psychic good health. The imaginary audience is narrowed
down to become one single person, the person watching the set.
For this reason, you find yourself being more available and more
open.

Besides, I have realised that I always express myself best in the
same way, through images. I don't believe that television in itself
has anything particularly sacred about it, just because it happens.
The particular aspect of expression through television - that is, the
unrepeatable image taken from among millions of coincidences -
should be used only to form a subjective reality. Otherwise - take
this garden, for instance - photographed just as it is now - it would
express nothing of what I myself would project into it.

It must be admitted, too, that in television language is much more important than images.

However, for the private reason I have mentioned, I wanted to work in television. Television is a medium in which I can work easily. The team is smaller than it is in the cinema, the whole thing suggests that it can be done quite easily.

I should like to meet producers who would let me make films without signing them: without false expectations, and without the promise of having to live up to them.

The fact is, I don't know quite how to deal with the problem of television. To me, it is just another way of working in the cinema: just as Picasso makes ceramics when he stops painting pictures for a while. Television can sprinkle a kind of freshness over anyone threatened by routine, or incipient hardening of the artieries, or a tendency to identify himself with the image which others have made of him. It is a way of getting out of the house and walking around the back lanes. It needs more money spent on it, though. Yet this lack of money is not really harmful. Italians are wonderfully fertile when they have to improvise. They are born improvisers, their psychic condition is formed that way.

At the beginning of this new job, I started off with the best intentions to make a serious inquiry. Then, I finished the inquiry. But I felt I had been rather clumsy. The fact is, I don't know how to ask questions. And if I venture to ask a question, I'm not really interested in the answer. As I went on with the inquiry, I showed how uneasy I felt.

Besides, in making an inquiry, there's always a pinch of the policeman peering into other people's private affairs, which worries me. Years ago I did something similar in the episode in *Amore in città*. The only way you can make an inquiry is by being rude, insolently nosey. And so there was a clearly satirical side to my inquiry, which allowed me to survive.

Let me say it again: the only documentary that anyone can make is a documentary on himself. 'The only true realist is the visionary': who said that? The visionary, in fact, bears witness to happenings which are his own reality, that is, the most real thing that exists. The trip to Paris was useful not because of the truth the inquiry might reveal, but because it allowed me to make a parody of an inquiry. It is always important to achieve one's own feeling for a thing. Then, one can also seek the comfort of having this confirmed by outside events.

All in all, the accusation made years ago, that I am a great

120

mystifier, may actually seem to be true.

The annunciation made to Federico

The reader must not expect a historical or philological treatise on the circus and on clowns in this book. Nor must he expect it from the film I made for television. My commitment to things is always subjective and emotional. If I go around looking at things, it is only to check up on what I have invented.

If pressed to do so, I might say that clowns - these grotesque, off-beat versions of drunkards, gossip-mongers, tramps - in their complete irrationality, their violence and their abnormal whims, are an apparition from my childhood, a prophecy, the anticipation of my vocation, 'the annunciation made to Federico'.

How is it that I already know all about the circus, about its innermost recesses, its lights, its smells?

I know it. I have always known it.

The circus isn't just a show, it is an experience of life. It is a way of travelling through one's own life. Obviously connections exist. How, otherwise, can you explain the way in which a child, when taken to church, may feel a sort of wild glory and become a priest, whereas I always feel cold there?

There's something of the madhouse in a circus. There's madness in it, and terrifying experiences. Yet the big top, and that smell of animals, is somehow familiar to me.

The threat of death, the feeling aroused by such shows, is connected with that felt in the ancient Circus Maximus in Rome.

There's blood on the sawdust.

Question: how could you find your vocation in something that you say was at first terrifying?

I can answer that at once: it was just because I felt myself immediately *inside* such a show that I was able to hold on to my emotion, that I felt a sort of terror unlike that of an ordinary spectator.

Of course, everything has already been said about the circus. It has become inflated, soused in literary allusions. All the same, and in spite of that, it exists and has a definite centre: it has its own dimensions, its own authentic atmosphere which cannot be put away in mothballs or hard covers, which never gathers dust because it is a way of life, a way of representing itself, which has gathered together within itself, in an exemplary way, certain lasting myths:

121

'. . . stepping into the limelight . . .' (8½)

adventure, travel, risk, danger, speed, stepping into the limelight . . .
and, at the same time, there is the more mortifying aspect of it
which keeps recurring, the fact that people come to see you and
you must exhibit yourself; that they examine you in this monstrous
way and have this biological, racial right to come and say: 'Well,
here I am, make me laugh, excite me, make me cry.' I think that
the circus, in spite of some obvious discrepancies between it and
the contemporary world, should be rescued. It is not out of date;
far more so are things like melodrama and revue. Obviously there
is something disproportionate between the effort it takes to bring
thirty elephants from Milan to Catania and the show you will have
from them when you get there. The circus still bases part of its
wonder on such exotic things (Indian or African animals, say), and
on danger, at a time when, in our cunning society, we can see any
natural spectacle close to on television or in the cinema, and can
take part in journeys to the moon.

And yet, notwithstanding this old-fashioned effort to astonish, the part which most struck us as children (the big top, the ring, the lights, the band) may remain as the background, the physical setting against which to express our ideas and our feelings. I was tempted to make a circus story out of the circus itself. The first part of the show would be made up of certain famous bits - music and costumes from the old days and some famous clowns. The second would be about the present day. And on tour for a year . . .

In other words, I find the circus congenial. Immediately I saw it I felt ecstatic, totally committed to that noise and music, to those monstrous apparitions, to those threats of death. In short, I can say that this type of show, based on wonder and fantasy, on jokes and nonsense, on fables and on the lack of any coldly intellectual meaning, is just the thing for me.

The fact that I have thrown an aura of death over the circus and its clowns is a proof of their vitality within me. When someone says 'God is death', it means merely that the demand for God is seen in a purer, more uncorrupted form than usual.

The clown is like a shadow

Panzini's *Modern Dictionary* gives the following definition of the clown:

'Clown: English word meaning *rustic, rough, clumsy*, later used to mean a man who made an audience laugh with contrived clumsiness. He is the Italian *pagliaccio*. But there is the usual distinction of meaning between our own and the foreign word. The English meaning raises the word higher than ours: the *pagliaccio* belongs to fairs and market places, the *clown* to circuses and theatres. A good acrobat is a *clown*, that is, almost an artist, and he would think it unsuitable and insulting to be called a *pagliaccio*. In the metaphorical sense, too, *clown* is the usual word. Even Carducci did not disdain to use it in his polemical prose works.'

Those were nationalistic times. What is there left for me to say?

Well then, the clown is the incarnation of a fantastic creature who expresses the irrational aspect of man; he stands for the instinct, for whatever is rebellious in each one of us and whatever stands up to the established order of things. He is a caricature of man's childish and animal aspects, the mocker and the mocked. The clown is a mirror in which man sees himself in a grotesque, deformed, ridiculous image. He is man's shadow. And so he will be forever. It is as if we were to ask ourselves: 'Is death the shadow? Does the shadow die?' For the shadow to die, the sun must be directly above our heads; then the shadow vanishes. The completely enlightened man has made his grotesque, ridiculous, deformed aspects disappear. Faced with so well-finished a creature, the clown - seen as his crippled aspect - would have no reason to exist. But the clown will not vanish, that's for sure. He will be merely assimilated. In other words, the irrational, the childish and the instinctive will no longer be seen with an eye that deforms them, that makes them deformed.

Wasn't St Francis known as God's clown? And didn't Lao Tse say: 'As soon as you have made a thought, laugh at it'?

The white clown and the fool

When I say clown, I think of the Auguste. The two types of clown are in fact the white clown and the Auguste. The white clown stands for elegance, grace, harmony, intelligence, lucidity, which are posited in a moral way as ideal, unique, indisputable divinities. Then comes the negative aspect, because in this way the white clown becomes Mother and Father, Schoolmaster, Artist, the Beautiful, in other words *what should be done*. Then the Auguste, who would feel drawn to all these perfect attributes if only they were not so priggishly displayed, turns on them.

The Auguste is the child who dirties his pants, rebels against this perfection, gets drunk, rolls about on the floor and puts up an endless resistance.

This is the struggle between the proud cult of reason (which comes to be a bullying form of aestheticism) and the freedom of instinct. The white clown and the Auguste are teacher and child, mother and small son, even the angel with the flaming sword and the sinner. In other words they are two psychological aspects of man: one which aims upwards, the other which aims downwards; two divided, separated instincts.

My film ends with the two figures meeting and going off together. Why is such a situation so moving? Because the two figures embody a myth which lies in the depths of each one of us: the reconciliation of opposites, the unity of being.

The painfulness which lies in the continual war between the white clown and the Auguste is not due to the music or anything of that kind, but to the fact that we are shown something that

124

embodies our incapacity to reconcile the two figures. The more I try to make the Auguste play the violin, the more he hiccups on the trombone. The white clown tries to make the Auguste elegant. But the more authoritatively he tries, the more ragged, clumsy and dusty the other becomes. It is the perfect image of an education that shows life in idealised and abstract terms. Lao Tse says: 'If you make a thought (= the white clown), laugh at it (= the Auguste).'

This is the moment to mention the popular and famous Chinese antithesis between *yin* and *yang*, cold and the sun, female and male, all possible opposites. I might talk of Hegel and dialectics, and say that perhaps the Auguste is an image of the sub-proletariat: the hungry, the lame, the rejected, those capable of revolt perhaps but not of revolution. Ordinary people have probably always treated him with familiarity because, being poor themselves, they have always felt pretty much at ease with the alarming.

The famous clowns, the Fratellini brothers introduced a third character, who was like the Auguste, but supported the boss. He was the bribed beggar, the copper's nark, the freed slave who lived between the two camps, halfway between authority and villainy.

In real life - with the exception of François Fratellini, who was an acrobatic white clown, full of grace and kindness, incapable of the harsh tone used in their act - all the white clowns were very hard men. It was said of Antonet, a famous white clown, that outside the ring he never spoke to Beby, who was his Auguste. The character influenced the man and vice versa.

Le clown blanc doit être mauvais: that is a rule of the game.

Auguste	:	I'm thirsty.
White clown	:	Have you any money?
Auguste	:	No.
White clown	:	Then you aren't thirsty.

Another tendency of the white clown is to take advantage of the Auguste, not just as a target for his jokes but as a servant, to do the chores. He sends him to fetch chairs, then puts a candle under his behind.

In other words, the white clown is a bourgeois, in his appearance as in everything else. He is startlingly splendid, rich and powerful. His face is white and ghostly, his haughty eyebrows are eloquently used, and his mouth is a single hard, cold, unattractive line. White clowns have always rivalled one another in the luxury of their dress. Theodore was a very famous one, who had a costume for each day of the year.

The Auguste, on the contrary, is always the same type. He never changes his clothes, can never change them. He is the tramp, the child, ragged and dirty.

The bourgeois family is a group of white clowns, in which the child is put into the position of the Auguste. The mother says: 'Do this, don't do that.' When the neighbours come in and the child is asked to recite a poem ('Show the ladies and gentlemen . . .'), you have a typical circus situation.

It's good for your health to be a clown

The white clown frightens children because he stands for duty, or, to use a fashionable term, repression.

The child, on the contrary, identifies at once with the Auguste, who, like the gosling or the puppy, is always ill-treated, and breaks plates, rolls on the floor, throws buckets of water in people's faces. In other words, he does everything the child would like to do and is prevented from doing by the various adult white clowns like his mother and his aunts.

In the circus, thanks to the Auguste, the child can imagine himself doing everything he is forbidden to do. He can dress up as a woman, make faces, yell in public, and say just what he thinks out loud. No-one condemns him; on the contrary, he gets clapped for it.

The old clown Bario spoke at length on tape about the liberating aspect of the Auguste's role in the circus. Sick, and scared of the lights, the old man was unable to repeat for the cameras what he had said in the earlier interview. Here are Bario's words - surprising, pathetic and profoundly true - as they were set down in the screenplay for the film:

SCENE 43
Circus ring. Interior. Night.
Against a dark, neutral background, Bario, in the foreground, speaks into a microphone.
BARIO: If you ask me what I think . . . well, I can't really say. Because I've known so many clowns, and nearly all of them made people laugh; but it's all been such a long time, and in these last few years I'm not sure that the audiences laugh the way they used to, any more. I used to make them laugh a lot myself, with my brother Dario, and Rhum, and my sons Nello and Freddy . . . we had an act with a cake inside a hat - oh, that was very, very funny! Everyone roared with laughter when we came into the ring. Once in Barcelona a piece of the trapeze fell on to my back and everyone laughed,

and I carried on with my number, with a broken collar-bone. The audience in Moscow were very nice. It was in Moscow we were told a tiger had got loose, but we mustn't say anything because people were there to enjoy themselves, so we went on with the number for nearly an hour, till the tiger was caught and we could leave the ring. No, I don't think it's all over and done with. Children love the circus . . . I come from Livorno, our surname is Meschi. I was working until a few years ago, but then - well, I'm getting on. Still, I think I could do something for the circus, even now. For instance, I could teach. I think a school for clowns would be very useful. The world's changed so much you need schools and teaching. Without it, youngsters will never become real clowns. They have to get used to running and climbing and jumping. Behind every clown there's an acrobat. If you're not an acrobat, you can't fall properly; and a good fall makes everyone laugh, even today. No money, of course. But the state ought to consider opening a school for clowns. No age limit: when a man's got the vocation for it, he can dedicate himself to it even at forty, and become a clown. Take an engineer, say. Now if he has the vocation for it, he can become a clown. University graduates, doctors, lawyers. They've all been excellent. Then there's make-up . . . Now, that has to be taught. Not too little and not too much. If it's too much, it scares the children. Take Albert Fratellini: he scared a lot of kids with his trombone and his feet that lit up like fireflies, and went on and off. It's good for your health to be a clown, you know. It's good because you can do anything you like: break everything, tear everything, set fire to things, roll on the floor, and nobody ticks you off, nobody stops you. The children wish they could do whatever they liked: tear things, set fire to things, roll on the floor . . . and so they love you. We ought to support them, and encourage them to go ahead with a good school for clowns, open to children - particularly to children. That way they could do what they liked, enjoy themselves and give enjoyment to others. It's a good job, and if you can do it you earn just as much as you would in an office. Why do parents want their children to work in offices and not be clowns? It's all wrong. People say: laughter is good for you. Oh, I agree. When a man's spent his life in the midst of laughter, then even when he's old his lungs are still full of oxygen . . . The best clowns are Italian or Jewish. Or Spanish. Have you ever seen the Rudi-Llattas? . . . Yes, on the whole I feel confident. I believe in a new circus, above all in a school, a school for clowns where I should love to teach - modestly, of course . . . Dario and I invented dozens of 'entrées'. The Bee, the Trombones, the Fake Doctor, the Singing Lesson, the Daughter of the Regiment, the Performing Dog; and then the Burning of Rome, the Drunk, the Woman in a Balloon . . . oh, there were such a lot, and lots of clowns copied them after us. I remembered one called the Death of a Clown . . . It made people laugh and it made them a little moved as well, particularly the women . . . We pretended that one of us was dead: sometimes me, sometimes Dario or Nello. The others were all crying, of course . . . And then I'd go look for him - looking for the dead man, that is. I'd look round, like this, and say: 'But where have you gone? Can you hear me? Even if you're dead, you're bound to be somewhere! Aren't you? A man can't just disappear!' And then at the end I'd pick up my trumpet . . . (*Bario picks up a trumpet.*)
. . . And, as if to try and cheer myself up, I'd start playing. It was as if I

127

wanted to wave for the last time to my dead friend, if you see what I mean . . .
Like this . . .
(Bario begins to play the trumpet. From high up, from some unspecified part of the big top, the sound of another trumpet answers him.
Bario plays on.
The other trumpet answers, slightly closer: little by little we come to see the other clown, who is youngish, with an expression of rather stupid content-ment, playing the trumpet as he gradually approaches Bario, as if answering his call.
Bario plays, and the other clown replies as he comes nearer. In the end, the two of them are standing in the ring, playing and walking slowly, still drawing closer together. Before they actually meet, darkness comes down on the ring, and the notes of the two trumpets die away.)

My home town becomes a big top

When the circus arrived at night, the first time I saw it as a child, it was like an apparition. There was a kind of balloon, preceded by nothing. The previous evening it hadn't been there, and in the morning there it was, right opposite our house. Immediately I thought it was some kind of oddly-shaped boat. This meant that the invasion - because of course there must have been an invasion - had something to do with the sea. Some small band of pirates, I supposed.

Then, quite apart from my terror, there was the deciding factor of the clown, who loomed fascinatingly up out of this marine atmosphere. The first clown, Pierino, was actually at the fountain, the morning after the show, and I saw him. Think of being able to touch him, of actually being him! Toto, his brother, was a poor white clown who wore a shirt and tie and fustian trousers in the ring. Making people laugh seemed to me simply splendid: a privilege, a piece of luck.

At the Sunday afternoon show, without the big top, near the prison, the convicts yelled behind their bars. A couple of times Toto, the white clown, behaved towards them as a white clown always behaves towards the unfortunate.

From that moment on, my home town imperceptibly became a big top. In this big top there were the Augustes, and with them the white clowns - which meant the fascist officials and bigwigs.

The fear which the clowns aroused (the Augustes in particular, the white clowns rather less) could be found, too, in certain scary local figures. Some of these characters were used to frighten us at home. 'If you don't eat up your spinach you'll end up like Giudizio,'

my mother used to say. Giudizio was the complete Auguste. He
wore a military overcoat five or six times too big for him, white
canvas shoes even in winter, and a horse-blanket over his shoulders;
and he had a dignity that was all his own, like all the raggedest
clowns. This dignity appeared in the most outlandish ways. He
would look at a gleaming car like an Isotta Fraschini and, holding
a cigarette stub to his mouth on a pin, say: 'I wouldn't have it as
a present!'

The white clown, on the other hand, with his moonlit charm
and unearthly midnight elegance, reminded me of the cold authority
of some of the nuns who had run nursery schools; or else of certain
stout fascists, in their gleaming black silk, their gilt epaulettes,
their whips (just like the clown's bat), their big overcoats, their
fezzes and their military medals; men who were still young but
had the pale faces of sleep-walkers or inhabitants of the underworld.

There were plenty of clowns about: Nasi, Fafinon, Bestemmia,
Dora and Gradisca, about whom I wrote in 'Rimini, my home
town'.

'That reminds me', people say to me; 'clowns are male as a rule,
but the most important clown figures in your films so far have
been women, Gelsomina and Cabiria. How is this?'

The only great female clown recorded in real life is Miss Lulu.
Gelsomina and Cabiria, in my films, are both Augustes. They are
not women, they are asexual; they are the Happy Hooligan from
the strip cartoon. The clown is sexless. Has Grock a sex? Has
Charlie Chaplin, even? I saw *The Circus* recently, a true masterpiece.
But Chaplin isn't at all the pathetic little man people talk about.
He is a happy cat who shrugs his shoulders and slinks off. Laurel
and Hardy sleep together. They are a pair of innocent Augustes,
absolutely lacking any sexual character at all. This was the very
reason they made people laugh.

The white clown v. the Auguste

The world, and not just Rimini, is full of clowns.

When I was in Paris doing the research for this film, I imagined
a sequence which was never filmed, in which we would drive round
in a taxi talking of clowns, and end up seeing them in the streets.
Ridiculous old women wearing absurd little hats, women holding
plastic handbags over their heads to keep off the rain, business men
in bowlers, and an embalmed-looking bishop in a car beside ours.

When I imagine myself as a clown, I'm an Auguste. But a white clown too. Or perhaps I'm the ring-master. The lunatics' doctor, himself a lunatic!

Let's take it further. Carlo Emilio Gadda is a fine Auguste; Guido Piovene, on the other hand, is a white clown. Alberto Moravia is an Auguste who would like to be a white clown. Or rather, he's Monsieur Loyal, the ring-master, who tries to reconcile the two tendencies in himself on an objective, impartial level. Pasolini is a white clown of the graceful, pretentious kind. Antonioni is one of those sad, silent, speechless Augustes. Goffredo Parise can be both: a tramp-like Auguste, always a little tipsy, but also a sharp, unpleasant, misogynous white clown, the sort that hits the Auguste without even explaining why. Picasso? A triumphant Auguste, brazen, without complexes, able to do anything: in the end he triumphs over the white clown. Einstein: a dreamy Auguste, entranced, saying nothing, but at the last minute he innocently pulls out of his bag the solution to the problem given him by the white clown. Visconti: a white clown with great authority, whose sumptuous costume alarms people from the start. Hitler: a white clown. Mussolini: an Auguste. Pope Pacelli: a white clown. Pope Roncalli: an Auguste. Freud: a white clown. Jung: an Auguste.

This game is so true that if you have a white clown with you, you are bound to play the Auguste, and vice versa.

The station-master in my film was a white clown. So we all became Augustes. Only when a more sinister white clown appeared - the fascist, that is - did we turn into white clowns ourselves, and then everybody ended up answering in a disciplined way with the Roman salute.

Only the ramshackle appearance of Giovannone, the Auguste who terrified the peasant women by exposing his penis like a dead hare (he exposed it as if astonished to be living with this lodger to whom he had given shelter), turned us into white clowns, when we said: 'But what are you up to, Giovannone?'

Even at Mass there was the same sort of relationship between the priest and certain hangers-on who wandered among the pews - boss-eyed and drunk - disturbing the service and asking for alms.

List of omissions

I clowns is now made. Some things - certain episodes - I didn't use, for one reason or another. For example, the clowns' shoemaker, in Paris:

SCENE 28
Shoemaker's shop. Paris. Exterior. Daytime.
The exterior of the shoemaker's shop, with clowns' big shoes on show.
Inside, a glimpse of the shoemaker, standing, talking to Fellini, seated.
Inside the shop. The shoemaker is talking about Rhum, and imitates his
gestures.
SHOEMAKER: Like this . . . He took the plate like this . . . Terrible! Rhum
was terrible. Of all the clowns I ever saw, he was the greatest. Very gentlemanly,
very careful . . . He did this . . . And grabbed the plate! Pity he drank; drank
a lot . . . He died quite young.
(Fellini examines some gigantic shoes.)
FELLINI: But now you must have less work, as clowns have almost disap-
peared.
SHOEMAKER: I've got too much work. I make shoes for revues, for trans-
vestites.
FELLINI: Transvestites?
SHOEMAKER: Yes. The other day - it's incredible. A chap came in to see me . . .
I was working here . . . I saw a pair of women's shoes coming up to me - shoes
I'd made myself.
(We see what the shoemaker is talking about. At the bottom of the door, we
see a pair of feet wearing women's shoes. The door is pushed open, and a
bearded young man comes in, wearing women's clothes.)
SHOEMAKER: Can you beat it? Wearing a beard and my shoes! Oh, there's
clowns enough, I can tell you . . .

Or else: still in Paris, the Medrano circus, turned into a beer-hall.

SCENE 29
The Medrano circus, Paris. Interior. Daytime. Afternoon.
The Medrano circus, turned into a beer-hall, in the morning or afternoon,
when there is no-one there. A group of waiters chatting in a corner, seated.
All the tables laid.
VOICE: The Medrano circus, perhaps the most famous in Europe, is no
longer a circus, but a Bavarian beer-hall. Let us look, in a melancholy way,
at the waiters laying the tables . . .
(A waiter approaches, carrying a tall pile of plates with some difficulty.)
. . . and for a moment imagine that even today, there are certain clownish
possibilities.
(The waiter trips and falls, breaking the plates as he might in a comic routine.
The boss, a little man with a moustache, rushes out and starts scolding the
waiter. The waiter runs away, shelters behind the buffet table, picks up a
cream pudding and hurls it . . . into the boss's face.
Mayhem breaks out, with cream cakes flying into faces and everything
upside down: ridiculous in that middle-European atmosphere.)

Or again: the clowns' photographer.

SCENE 30

Photographer's studio. Paris. Interior. Daytime.
The office of a specialist photographer. The photographer, his fingers stained
with acid, is running through photographs of old clowns. As he does so he
murmurs quietly.
PHOTOGRAPHER: This is all I've got left. This is Rastelli. This is Porto.
Pipo and Rhum. Final line-up at the Cirque d'Hiver.
(Fellini looks at the photographs. Then he speaks.)
FELLINI: Rhum . . . Do you think he was one of the greatest clowns? Or
even the very best?
PHOTOGRAPHER: Well . . . he made people laugh a lot, certainly . . . At the
Medrano. But when left the Medrano, nobody laughed at all. He was a
drunkard. Every evening he emptied a bottle of red wine while he was making
up. Truly. Sometimes his partner had to hold him up to stop him falling.
But then it would pass. Afterwards, he'd be all right. Yes, he made people
laugh a lot. I remember him . . .
FELLINI: But why did he drink?
(The photographer shrugs his shoulders and looks rather nostalgically at a
large photo of Rhum.)
PHOTOGRAPHER: Love, I think. Troubles in love. He was madly in love
with a little actress. Ugly as sin. And she was unfaithful to him. She used to
say: 'You're ugly! You're much too ugly.' He was called Enrico Sprocani.
FELLINI: Who, Rhum?
PHOTOGRAPHER: Sure. His real name was Enrico Sprocani. I think he was
Italian.

Finally: the Kafkaesque tirade of the elephant tamer at the
Cirque d'Hiver (a piece of abstract information in statistical terms,
as you will see: 'Enthusiasm for elephants has declined a great deal
these past few years . . .').

SCENE 32

Cirque d'Hiver. Paris. Interior. Daytime.
The great seraglio-like hall of the Cirque d'Hiver. The elephants, in a row,
move their heads rhythmically, including a small elephant at the end of the
line. Assistants wearing boots are busy to no discernible purpose. In a cage
are strange little animals, among them a small pink pig and several chickens.
VOICE: The Cirque d'Hiver still carries on, but only three days a week. The
enclosure, which is as big as a hangar, smells like a stable, a zoo, or an arena.
Here, too, the atmosphere is that of a party which is over, of an out-of-date
show. Let's hear what the old elephant trainer has to say.
(The old trainer goes across to the elephants and as he does so talks softly,
as if ashamed.)
TRAINER: Enthusiasm for elephants has declined a great deal these past
few years. I can remember when shouts and applause used to greet the
elephants when they came into the ring, and the more sensitive ladies would
even feel ill, and faint. Today, the elephants come in, go round, and do their
turn to a bored audience that doesn't love them any more, doesn't participate,

132

isn't moved. And yet elephants . . . Well, you know, they're not like other animals. They're intelligent, wise, they understand everything, they're real professionals, proper show-business people. If one of the benches is crooked, they push it straight with their trunks. And they think deeply, wisely, intelligently. After all these years I've learned their language a little. Not their trumpetings, of course, but their thoughts. Why, of course the elephant thinks . . . Look at this one here. See his little eye? See how reproachful he looks? He's jealous. Certainly he is. He looks at me and tries to say: Today you washed the other elephants better than me. And it's true . . . Yes, I gave the others a shower, but him I gave just a lick and a promise - we ran out of water . . .

(The trainer puts a few sugar lumps in his hand and the elephant takes them with his trunk. The trainer smilingly strokes the elephant, and murmurs some incomprehensible words to him, which the elephant seems to understand. There is no-one in the ring of the Cirque d'Hiver. A ray of sunlight comes in, a pigeon flies among the seats. Fellini and some of his team are sitting on the edge of the ring, silent as if they were in church, waiting.)

VOICE: The owner of the Cirque d'Hiver, Mr Buglione, had agreed to meet us, but was late. We felt as if we were in church, as if the dove was fluttering above something holy. In photographs taken during the Belle Epoque, the Cirque d'Hiver looks larger, glittering with lights and elegant women. Today it has shrunk into a little circus. Its audience consists almost entirely of children.

(Mr Buglione appears and pauses on the threshold: serious, suspicious, hard, in a big black hat. Fellini goes up to him, talks to him, gesturing at things around them. Buglione listens unsmilingly, staring at the floor or ahead of him.)

BUGLIONE: Oui, ça c'est possible . . .

(While the members of Fellini's team are preparing to put across the atmosphere of the circus, two young men come in, carrying bundles; they talk very deferentially to Buglione.)

VOICE: Buglione, ex-animal tamer and an authoritarian man, is the last representative of the race of traditional circus owners. He is now getting ready to audition two young clowns who have come to see him, hoping to be taken on.

(Buglione stands at the entrance, smoking, and looks coldly at the two young men. Just as they are, in their overcoats and scarves, the pair of them start their number, which is hesitant, uncertain, bitter. One of them has a guitar, the other an enormous violin case.)

ONE: What have you got in there?

TWO: A violin.

(Two opens the case and takes out a minute violin. One is amazed.)

ONE: D'you call that a violin?

TWO: Well, it's the son of a violin. It's only three months old, but it'll grow.

(Fellini and his team watch without laughing, feeling almost moved.)

ONE: Right then, let's play. I'll accompany you.

TWO: Where?

ONE: Nowhere! I'll accompany you on this.

(He shows him the guitar.)

TWO: Ah! Is it a frying pan?

133

ONE: No, you idiot, it's a guitar.
TWO: Right. Then let's play, and I'll sing. Ladies and gentlemen, I'm now going to sing a modern song.
(*Two opens his mouth to sing, but stretches it too far, and stays like that, unable to shut it.*)
ONE: What's up? Can't you shut your mouth? Never mind, I'll fix it!
(*One bangs his guitar down on Two's head, and Two's mouth shuts. No-one is standing in the entrance any longer. Buglione has gone away in silence. The two young men make signs to each other, and stop. They put away their instruments and make ready to go.*)

The last part of this scene was later changed when I was able to introduce Chaplin's daughter into the film. We had even thought up a sequence for Chaplin himself, inspired by the tragic adventure of the rider Corradini. Corradini had an amazing number. He went into a lift with his horse: an enormous circus lift that carried up Corradini, in top hat and tails, riding Blonden, with his hooves on four discs the size of horseshoes. When he got near the dome of the big top, Corradini lit a series of coloured rockets, then he waved to the audience and came down.

One evening, a spark from one of the rockets flew into the horse's eye. He reared up on to his hind legs. Corradini knew the horse would never be able to bring his front hooves down on to the two small discs, and kept him on his hind legs, with his forelegs in the air for as long as he could. Then he stroked Blonden, waved his top hat at the audience, and plunged below on his horse, killing himself.

I wanted to reconstruct this event with Chaplin's help. But in the end I gave up the idea, as I didn't want to force him to refuse.

I also gave up the idea of telling the story of the Zacchini family, who invented the human cannon-ball. The human cannon-ball was shot out of the cannon's mouth, and, either because of the blow on his heels, or because of the powder mixture that had to make people believe he was being fired, for a while he would lose consciousness as he flew through the air. So he always had to recover consciousness a moment before landing, in order to make the vital jump that would allow him to fall into the safety net.

A whole series of deaths resulted from this number. Of the fifty-six human cannon-balls who performed it, thirty-two were killed.

In the end Zacchini made an aeroplane from which he emerged to do somersaults at a height of one to two hundred metres above

134

the ground. His wife sat in the cockpit, but didn't know how to work it. One day Zacchini fell to the ground, injuring himself, and his wife had to stay up, flying, until the petrol ran out.

In the United States, where they lived, the Zacchinis had a small house with a little garden, too small to train human cannon-balls. So, starting from the garden, they had to fire them across the road outside the house, landing them in a field beyond. Car drivers who didn't know this often had accidents when they saw men flying across the road; they thought they were having halluci-nations and lost control of their cars. So the mayor of Tampa, the small town where the Zacchinis lived - which considered them a local marvel, like the Eiffel Tower - at last put up notices at either end of the road: 'If you see a flying man, do not be alarmed. It is just the Zacchinis rehearsing their stunts.'

Another scene which remained unused was one about an imperti-nent microphone. An animated microphone - an Auguste - refuses to broadcast what a white clown says, and stands up to him by twisting itself around him, laughing openly at him, and making snide remarks about what he is saying.

It was an old idea I had had when I was young: the idea that the microphone, by bleating and putting out wrong news items, would revolt against the dreary rubbish it was made to broadcast in fascist times. The director of Radio Igea at that time was a Dr Moschetto, who, when we showed him the little sketch, refused to pass it.

Of course, there is endless material on the circus. And so as to keep strictly to the subject of clowns I also cut from the first screenplay this crazy short sequence:

SCENE 33
A Swedish boarding house. Paris. Interior. Daytime.
Old Houcke, in an armchair, is smoking and sipping his coffee. He speaks forcefully and contemptuously.
HOUCKE: The young clowns no longer make people laugh! They make them cry!
FELLINI: And how old are you, Mr Houcke?
HOUCKE: Ninety two! I'm the oldest circus manager in the world! (*He laughs*). And I'm soon going to open a new circus! Le Cirque de l'Avenir!
FELLINI: Really? How interesting! And what will it be like, this circus of the future?
HOUCKE: Well, I've got lots of new ideas. For instance, I'll go to La Scala in Milan and put a famous singer under contract. Then I'll make a fine

carriage race round and round the ring with the tenor singing inside it . . .
(*Houcke starts to sing; his voice is well controlled, but tremulous and absurd.*)

SCENE 34
Circus ring. Carriage. Interior. Daytime.
Meantime, while Houcke is singing, lightly superimposed, as in a dream, we see the carriage and pair racing round a circus ring. A hallucination; a moment's madness.

Now I come to think of it, there are always so many things left out, so many that have to be sacrificed. The original sound-track, for instance, the one taken while the film is actually being made, and always a completely faithful private diary of the film, day by day: unexpected voices, wind, angry squalls from me, mistakes, hesitations, whole sequences of numbers instead of dialogue (for simplicity's sake) . . .

For instance: you see Terence Stamp (in a scene from *Toby Dammit*) crouched behind a table crowded with half-empty bottles. He is drunk, and looks around him with the restless, worried air of a neurotic. Campanella comes up to him (this is a piano-tuner I insist on using because he has a face that fascinates me), and with the knowing air of a Mafia man starts murmuring: One - two - three - four - five - six - seven - eight.
Terence Stamp, alarmed: Eight?
Campanella: Yessir! Eight!
Then he glances across at the camera, looks for me and mutters: Well, what do I do now?
Me: Go ahead, count up to 29, but a bit more gently.
Campanella, who is Neapolitan, makes a face that means 'Anything you say . . .' and carries on: Nine - ten - eleven - twelve . . . and so on, quietly. Terence Stamp then gets up, swaying, and starts reciting into the microphone in English: Out, out, brief candle! Life's but a walking shadow . . .

From numerical delirium to Shakespeare!

In *Satyricon*, Trimalcione beat all records by counting up to 138. But it was a very important scene and shooting it was a very long business.

Ruggero Mastroianni, my editor, says that an accountant or a computer would be very useful in the post-synching of my films. Of course I can't leave this arithmetical dialogue in the film, even though, as Zapponi maintains, in its absurd abstractness it sometimes seems more interesting than the finished copy. In the same

136

'Broderick Crawford, dying, alone, on the edge of a cliff . . .' (*Il bidone*)

way I cannot leave in all the casual, extraneous things that have
oddly managed to get on to the sound-track: a tram screeching
round a corner, a car jamming on its brakes, a child screaming
unconsolably in some house, or the voice of a woman saying firmly:
'Priscilla, I'm going to smack you!' Once, in *Il bidone*, when we
were projecting the day's rushes, underneath a dramatic scene
(Broderick Crawford dying, alone, on the edge of a cliff), we
suddenly heard: 'What do I care! You've got to let me go by!
Idiots, I'd like to have you all put in gaol!' It was the usual
respectable gentleman who, while the scene was being filmed, had
been stopped in the street by some policeman or member of the
production team.

It really is sad to have to clean up the original sound-track, to
cut out the most intimate, unforeseeable, authentic moments in
the making of the film.

What else is left? Having admitted that one is right to ask
questions at the end of making a film, might not one ask more
pertinently: Is the film as it is made really the film one wanted to

137

'. . . the sense of play and at the same time of an execution . . .' (*I clowns*)

make? As far as I'm concerned, when the film is made and finished, I have no curiosity, I never go and check whether I said everything I had in mind to say or whether I said it as I meant to say it, whether by any chance I neglected or omitted anything. No, the finished film exists. I can't remember what I wanted to do in the first place, I don't know exactly what it was. And even if I happen to see the screenplay or the scribbles in which I first put down my filmic ideas, it seems as if they refer to some other film: the film I might have made, not the one I actually made.

Sometimes, at a distance of years, fragments from scenes loom up from nowhere, views of streets, expressions on faces, things said in silence, an indecipherable glance from some character . . . They are bits of the film as I wanted to make it, images I never realised but with which I lived for a long time before I began filming. They reappear unsought in the fluctuating, indefinite layer of memory, paler, more wan, cut to pieces, with the silent reproachfulness of ghosts that have never been given a body; and then vanish in silence as if swallowed up in the dark empty spaces of the imagination. They always leave me with a vague feeling of regret and remorse.

Will they appear again and become part of another film? Perhaps, completely transformed, unrecognisable.

Of course I always feel a doubt about this little film. Is the surprise, the feeling of bewilderment, of the unknown and at the same time the familiar, which I felt the first time I saw the clown Pierino - is all this in the film? Have I managed to tell it the way I wanted to? And what about the smell of sawdust, and of wild animals, the mysterious gloom up there under the dome of the big top, the heart-rending music, the sense of play and at the same time of an execution, of holiday and butchery, of grace and madness, all of which makes up the circus: has all this gone into my film?

[1970]

Comic-strip heroes

I began to understand the essence of what is comic when I was a child, in the comic-strips of Frederick Burr Opper and George McManus, *Happy Hooligan, Maud, Alphonse and Gaston* and *Bringing Up Father.* In those days they were published in Italy without balloons containing the dialogue, but with rhymes of a sort underneath the picture, rhymes that were never quite detailed enough - since, as we all know, rhymes may alter things a little. In other words, a fundamental part of the composition was missing: the text which is included in the image and forms part of the image itself. But, all the same, I did get an idea of this ingenious and already highly delicate art, and it even provided me with a way of looking at the world.

Then I discovered that comics also offered adventure. It is very hard to explain just how much the coming of Alexander Raymond's Flash Gordon meant to boys of my generation in Italy. When we began to read about the astounding adventures of this galactic hero, fascism was at its height, its gloomy, dreary rhetoric in full flood. Admittedly fascism kept calling us to bravery and daring, kept telling us of the need to fight and win, but what it said seemed boring rubbish, and the heroes it set before us were not the least bit attractive. Flash Gordon, on the other hand, seemed an unbeatable hero from the very beginning, a hero who belonged to real life even though his actions took place in distant, fantastic worlds.

I, and others of my age, have remained deeply attached to Flash

Gordon and his creator. When I think of him, I think of someone who really existed. At times in my films I have wished to use the colours which the Italian newspaper used in printing the Flash Gordon strips; strips that did have balloons but also several translation mistakes. For instance, when he first appeared on a Sunday picture page in 1934, Flash Gordon was introduced as a 'Yale graduate', whereas in the Italian version he was called a 'police officer'. The mistake was corrected only recently; I have a feeling that there is a big difference between the two - a substantial difference, in fact.

I am writing this not in order to talk about myself and risk being accused of writing my autobiography yet again, but simply to record my lasting interest in these comics, and my lasting gratitude to them. This interest and gratitude make me particularly like James Steranko's book, *History of Comics* [Super Graphics Publications, Reading, Penn., 1970], which contains not just the story of the comic-strip heroes but that of their creators, from Alex Raymond to Will Eisner and from Milt Caniff to Hal Foster . . . and on to Stan Lee and the revolution he brought about in comics. Stan Lee's revolution consisted in adding a comic vein to their adventures, or rather in establishing the essentially comic element in them.

Without ceasing to be heroes, indeed becoming progressively more heroic, the characters in the Marvel group of comics learnt to laugh at themselves. Their adventures were advertised with a sort of schoolboy megalomania and carried out in the strips themselves with a kind of mature masochism; and yet there was nothing devious about the result, which was a lively, aggressive, naughty, never-ending story that kept starting over and over again, not giving a damn if things happened to be puzzling or paradoxical. Puzzles and paradoxes, if cheerfully stood up to, never killed anyone. The only thing that kills is boredom. And boredom, luckily, is something that steers clear of these comics.

[1970]

'Whom do you most admire?'

Whom do you most admire, Federico, apart from yourself?

The good Lord. I feel he made things really well, in spite of what I've heard people say.

And after that?

Well, maybe everyone, maybe nobody. Joking apart, this admiration business can become really difficult for me, because I'm the sort of person who never makes eternal choices. I've always exaggerated a bit in giving my loyalty to someone, and the same thing happens when I suddenly take it away. I'm notorious for being struck by people, for falling in and out of love easily. How can one choose? Well, one criterion is that of cycles - stages in life. Yes, that's a good way of looking at it. There's the cycle of childhood, the cycle of youth, the cycle of maturity. My grandmother Franzscheina, the prostitute Gradisca, the clown Pierino, the heroes of Edgar Wallace, then my present-day comrades - Picasso, Jung, Moravia. Yes, you can do it that way. Making it clear that there are some people left off the list not because I don't admire them but because, on the contrary, I admire them constantly, lastingly . . .

For instance?

For instance, my lifelong companion, Giulietta Masina.

My Grandmother Franzscheina

My paternal grandmother, Franzscheina (the Romagna dialect version of Franceschina), was someone I admired enormously when

142

Fellini during the shooting of *Toby Dammit*

I was small. She always wore a black head-scarf and looked like the female counterpart of Chief Sitting Bull. She had a squaw's profile with a great hooked nose, a hard, clean-cut mouth and, in a network of white wrinkles on her sunburned face, a pair of gleaming, piercing little eyes. Franzscheina towered over my childhood like some legendary figure. She was a magnificent 'azdora' - that is, someone who really ruled, who carried burdens, who governed.

She always carried a cane with which she made the men jump as they might in a film cartoon. (I've told this story in the chapter on Rimini.) And she was remarkable with animals, too. She could guess their illnesses and their moods and attributed human characteristics to them: she would say a particular horse was a liar, a cow was jealous, a calf was crazy. She was always something of a seer, especially when it came to the weather. She could predict very far ahead: for instance when the wind was going to change direction. 'We shall have the *garbein* in a few days,' she would say. The *garbein* is an extra wind they get in Romagna. A whimsical, unstable, absolutely unpredictable wind. Unpredictable to everyone except Franzscheina.

The clown Pierino

I have already told of the first time I saw a circus and the first time I saw the clown, Pierino, at the fountain the morning after the show . . . There is no doubt at all that he was the first herald of my unmistakeable vocation. I have always been profoundly moved by the clochard, the clown, the vagabound who turns up shabbily dressed, playing the part of the orphan or the innocent victim; in other words, I have always been moved by everything unrespectable in this joyful, funny, ragged rogue who nevertheless arouses affection and applause. First Pierino, then Chaplin and all the others. I was moved and I admired the poor man dressed as a funny man, whom I realised was a free, amazing being, needing very little to live on and able to survive the most incredible disasters, able to rise from the most frightful calamities, pass unharmed through mockery and contempt and to the very end maintain an unflagging optimism: amused and amusing as only one under heaven's protection could possibly be.

From that first moment, I was totally fascinated by the clown. For he embodies, in a fantastic character, all the irrational aspects of man, the instinctive part of him, the touch of rebellion against

144

'I was totally fascinated by the clown . . .' (Fellini during the shooting of
I clowns)

the established order which is in each one of us. He is a caricature of the most animal, most childish aspects of man, the victim of jokes and the joker. From that very first meeting I wanted to be like him. And, basically, in the end I've succeeded.

Castrichella

Castrichella is a film extra. One of the many humble extras that have always followed me, that I have seen growing old, that I love to find over and over again in my films: gentle faces in which I project myself, faces with something familiar about them that represent my quirks and manias and oddities. In the end, I recognise myself in them and they become symbols of something in me, quite apart from the film. I could give their names, but these would mean nothing. All I need to know is that they are there, that they exist. I look after them, too, and help them, but not as a benefactor or a philanthropist. Rather with the besotted selfishness of a puppet-master in relation to his puppets.

In my work, and with my particular temperament, the relationship of liking and affection, of gratitude and loyalty, that binds me to these extras, to their anonymous, never emphasised presence, is very important. The extra is the human material I have chosen. Docile, modest, humble, marvellously available for any imaginative variation - full colour or a mere outline, prince or pauper, minister or beggar. This liking of mine for the archetypal figure in my work may make me suspected of some sort of literary rhetoric; but it is authentic, true, and profound. Hurrah for all Castrichellas, those invaluable collaborators in my films!

Pablo Picasso

I have dreamt of Picasso three times. In the first dream (which was at a time of serious depression, of total lack of confidence) I remember that we were in a kitchen, obviously the kitchen of his house, a huge place crammed with food, pictures and paints. We talked all night. In the second dream (again at a time of great confusion and uncertainty) I saw him riding a horse, galloping along and jumping over every obstacle in an incredibly light, graceful and elegant way. Once again I dreamt of him, and once more it was in a time of profound uneasiness. This time there was a great stretch of sea, which looked to me as the sea looks from the port of

146

Rimini: a dark, stormy sky, with great green waves and the white horses on them that appear during storms. In front of me a man was swimming, with powerful strokes, his bald head poking up from the water, a small white fluff of hair on the back of his neck. Suddenly he turned towards me: it was Picasso, and he made me a sign to follow him further on, to a place where we should find good fishing.

No need to be a psycho-analyst to realise that I saw in Picasso a kind of tutelary deity, a charismatic presence, a genius in the mythological sense of the word - protective, nourishing, vital. To me Picasso is the eternal embodiment of the archetype of creativity as an end in itself, with no other motive, no other end, than itself - irruptive, unarguable, joyous.

I saw Picasso only once, at Cannes, when *Le notti di Cabiria* was being shown. He was dressed in his usual way, with a beret, an orange velvet jacket, a sailor's T-shirt and shorts. Someone introduced us but in the hurly-burly we could not manage to talk.

Carl Gustav Jung

I have complete faith in Jung, and total admiration for him. Ernst Bernhard, a psycho-analyst who lived in Rome and whom I was lucky enough to know, explained his thought to me in an incomparable way. When I speak briefly of Jung, I feel I am inevitably failing to do justice to the depth of this experience and to its determining effect upon me. How can I put it? It was like the sight of unknown landscapes, like the discovery of a new way of looking at life; a chance of making use of its experiences in a braver and bigger way, of recovering all kinds of energies, all kinds of things, buried under the rubble of fears, lack of awareness, neglected wounds.

What I admire most ardently in Jung is the fact that he found a meeting place between science and magic, between reason and fantasy. He has allowed us to go through life abandoning ourselves to the lure of mystery, with the comfort of knowing that it could be assimilated by reason. My admiration is the sort felt for an elder brother, for someone who knows more than you do and teaches it to you. It is the admiration we owe to one of the great travelling companions of this century: the prophet-scientist.

Alberto Moravia

In a country like ours, conditioned to superstition and sentimentality, to a foolish, vehement individualism, always prey to childish, immoderate, at best ritualistic feelings, and at the same time always liable to distort and, in an emotional way, amplify the facts and figures of reality, a mind that seeks to remain cool, lucid and well ordered like Moravia's seems to me comforting and reassuring, ready as it is to give a meaning to things and to treat them in a way that is human and useful.

What I like about Moravia is the way he suggests more adult and autonomous points of view and hypotheses than those we already know, and classifies experience in a more mature and useful way. He searches as a biologist might and does so even when he talks about himself; and he sees this strength and lucidity as a limitation within himself. Every now and then, a touch of melancholy appears in his rigorous, unwearied search, a hint of longing for a darker freedom; and this, I think, makes Moravia's choice a very careful, very human one, a moving challenge to the deceit and imperfection of feeling and fantasy.

Jorge Luis Borges

Borges always gives me a remarkable feeling of peace and exaltation because of his amazing ability to catch, if only for a moment, such rarefied and ambiguous things as time, destiny, death and dreams, in powerful, delicate mental operations, in vigorously simplified mental concepts, entirely lacking the glitter of logic or the balancing acts of dialectic. Borges is particularly stimulating to a man who works in the cinema, because the unusual thing about his writing is that it is like a dream, extraordinarily farsighted in calling up from the unconscious complete images in which the thing itself, and its meaning, coexist - exactly as happens in a film. And, just as happens in dreams, in Borges the incongruous, the absurd, the contradictory, the arcane and the repetitive, although as powerfully imaginative as ever, are at the same time illumined like the careful details of something larger, something unknown, and are the faultless elements of a cruelly perfect, indifferent mosaic. Even the fact that Borges's work is strangely fragmentary makes me think of a broken dreamlike flow; and the heterogeneous quality of his work - stories, essays, poems - I prefer to see not as the union of the multiple threads in a greedy, impatient talent, but as a mysterious sign of unending change.

[1972]

Miscellany III–
'I see no dividing line between imagination and reality'

1. **I am not a 'therapeutic' artist**, my films don't suggest solutions
or methods, they don't put forward ideologies. All I do is bear
witness to what happens to me, interpret and express the reality
that surrounds me. If, through my films - that is, recognising
themselves in them - people come to an equal awareness of themselves, then they have achieved the state of clear-sighted detachment from themselves which is essential in making new choices,
in bringing about changes.

2. **My films don't have what is called a final scene.** The story never
reaches its conclusion. Why? I think it depends on what I make of
my characters. It's hard to put it - but they're a kind of electrical
wire, they're like lights that don't change at all but show an
unchanging feeling in the director from start to finish. They cannot
evolve in any way; and that's for another reason. I have no intention
of moralising, yet I feel that a film is the more moral if it doesn't
offer the audience the solution found by the character whose story
is told. In other words, the man who has just seen a character
sorting out his problems, or becoming good when he started off
bad, finds himself in a much more comfortable situation. He is
going to say quietly to himself: 'Well, all I have to do is carry on
being the creep I am, betraying my wife, conning my friends,
because at a given moment the right solution will turn up, just as
it does in the films . . .' My films, on the contrary, give the audience
a very exact responsibility. For instance, they must decide what

Cabiria's end is going to be. Her fate is in the hands of each one of us. If the film has moved us, and troubled us, we must immediately begin to have new relationships with our neighbours. This must start the first time we meet our friends or our wife, since anyone may be Cabiria - that is, a victim. If films like *I vitelloni, La strada* and *Il bidone* leave the audience with this feeling, mixed with a slight uneasiness, I think they have achieved their object. I feel, and I can even say today, unhesitatingly, that whenever I think up a story it is in order to show some anxiety, some trouble, a state of friction in the relationships that ought normally to exist between people. If I were a political animal, in order to explain this I should hold meetings or join a political party; or go out barefoot and dance in the streets. If I had found a solution, and if I were able to explain it convincingly and in good faith, then of course I should not be a story-teller, or a film-maker.

3. Good intentions and honest feelings, and a passionate belief in one's own ideals, may make excellent politics or influential social work (things which may be much more useful than the cinema), but they do not necessarily and indisputably make good films. And there is really nothing uglier or drearier - just because it is ineffectual and pointless - than a bad political film.

4. Commitment, I feel, prevents a man from developing. My 'anti-fascism' is of a biological kind. I could never forget the isolation in which Italy was enclosed for twenty years. Today I feel a profound hatred - and I am actually very vulnerable on this point - for all ideas that can be translated into formulas. I am committed to non-commitment.

I love becoming committed to frivolous things. In fact, I am wholly committed to everything I do.

5. I am against things that try to define themselves too precisely, and against people who do the same. The word 'committed' irritates me. I react in a childish, exaggerated way to those who profess to be committed. People who are over forty-five today, you see, grew up in the shadow of fascism and the Church. All through my childhood, I heard things spoken of in terms of duty. Idealised commitment. Now, when I hear today's young people putting forward and developing the same sort of idiocy as Mussolini and the bishops, it really makes me mad.

151

I see in it a threat to true freedom. That is, authentic individual growth. What on earth is the 'committed cinema' committed to do? This kind of Marxist or Chinese terminology makes me very suspicious. Not because of what you might call individual anarchy, but because of what is really a personal experience.

Fascism meant omnipotent stupidity and ignorance. I cannot say that I ever fought in the anti-fascist ranks; that would not be true; I have never played at politics.

6. After the war, our subjects were handed to us, ready-made. There were very simple problems: how to survive, the war, peace. These problems were set before us, in an immediate, brutal way. But today the problems are different. Of course the neo-realists were not hoping that war and poverty would continue because they found their best subjects in them . . . but it sometimes seemed as if the neo-realists thought they could make a film only if they put a shabby man in front of the camera. They were wrong.

7. To me, neo-realism is a way of seeing reality without prejudice, without conventions coming between it and myself - facing it without preconceptions, looking at it in an honest way - whatever reality is, not just social reality, but spiritual reality, metaphysical reality, all that there is within a man . . . In telling the story of particular people I always try to show a particular truth.

8. Realism is a bad word. In a certain sense everything is realistic. I see no dividing line between imagination and reality. I see a great deal of reality in imagination. I don't feel it's my responsibility to arrange everything neatly on one universally valid level. I have an infinite capacity for amazement, and I don't see why I should set up a pseudo-rational screen to protect me from being amazed.

9. Realism is neither a tight enclosure nor a one-dimensional panorama. A landscape, for instance, has a number of layers, and the deepest, which only poetic language can reveal, is not the least real. What I want to show beyond the outer surface of things is what people call 'unreal'. They say I have a taste for mystery. If they liked to give the word a capital M, then I would be glad to accept it. To me, mysteries belong to man, they are the great unreasoning lines of his spiritual life, love, health . . . At the centre of successive layers of reality, God is to be found, I think - the key

'I see no dividing line between imagination and reality' (*I clowns*)

to the mysteries. I would add that if neo-realism is called 'social', as it is by certain Italian critics, then it is limited. Man is not just a social being, he is divine.

10. I am not yet humble enough to make myself an abstraction in my films. I try in them to throw light on what I don't understand in myself, but as I am a man, other men can no doubt see themselves in the same mirror too. What is autobiographical is the story of a kind of call that pierces the torpor of the soul and wakes me. I should very much like to stay in that state, in those moments when the call reaches me. I feel, then, that someone is knocking at the door and I don't go and open it. Of course I shall have to make up my mind to open it, some day or other. Basically, I must be a spiritual *vitellone.*

11. In my way of thinking, there do not exist humorous themes or themes which are not humorous. Humour, just like the dramatic, the tragic, the visionary, is the collocation of reality in a particular climate. Humour is a type of view, of rapport, of feeling one has about things, and is, above all, a natural characteristic which one has or doesn't have. In this sense, to speak of utilising the humorous to balance certain atmospheres or situations, tends to suggest, even though vaguely, an idea of premeditation, of calculated dosing, something which is absolutely extraneous to the whole phenomenon of humour, in fact the very negation of it.

12. When Rossellini said that *La dolce vita* **was the film of a provincial**, he didn't realise what he was saying, since my own feeling is that to call an artist provincial is the best way of defining him. For an artist's position in the face of reality must be exactly that of a provincial, he must be attracted by what he sees and at the same time have the detachment of a provincial. What is an artist, in fact? He is merely a provincial who finds himself standing between a physical and a metaphysical reality. Faced with a metaphysical reality, we are all provincials. Who then is a citizen of the transcendent world? . . . The saints. But it is the no-man's-land that I call provincial, the frontier between the world of the senses and the suprasensible world, that is truly the artist's kingdom.

13. I have read *The Students' Little Red Book* and my reactions to it are subjective, related directly to my own experience of school. To me and, I imagine, to everyone else of my generation, school was dark, sad and unreal; unreal in the sense of life-denying, in the sense that it showed all the truest and solidest things in life in a completely dead, abstract sort of way. It was therefore, profoundly, a non-education. Then there was the sense of guilt, and embarrassment, of underlying, corrosive fear, the frustrating sense that time spent in class was all wasted. There were the passages and classrooms, evil-smelling and steeped in a feeling of grim inertia. I remember certain kindly, innocent teachers as outlandish and crazy, as heartrendingly cruel. If I now think back to all that, then the pages of this manual of schoolboy revolt put me into a remarkably good humour, very cheerfully on their side.

In those days it would have been as inconceivable as it was impossible to stand up to the school establishment with such lucid, culturally well organised criticisms, with so much self awareness, such a simple, confident knowledge of one's own individual nature, and with such a natural and accurate grasp of the problems, contradictions and evils of school - and not merely of school. Indeed some paragraphs in the *Little Red Book* have so detached, ironic, amused and adult a tone that I have been a little worried by it, as one is when faced with something completely new and strange.

It may be that something as brave and sincere as the publication of this book may be used as a tool for demagogy, as a means of spreading anonymous and uncritical confusion. But I don't feel that a possibility of this kind should make us ignore, or worse still silence, the authentic demands of freedom and maturity which the *Little Red Book* expresses.

14. Today's cinema seems to me in the same situation as that of all the other art forms. A very odd situation. This situation is diagnosed all over the world (while the amazing, indeed cancerous, growth of reasons social, political, ethical and aesthetic which actually account for it are neglected) as being a classic one of confusion, impotence, emptiness, crises, transition, and the abolition of all the rules and values that existed until our time. I think there is something very seriously wrong with this diagnosis. It seems to me the result of value judgements which, having shored up the diagnosis, ought to be thrown out with the rest. In short, we apply to the experiments and new expressions of any art form, including the cinema, an absolutely traditional critical criterion compounded of impotence, confusion and irrelevance. Basically, when faced with an abstract painting or an anti-novel, with pop art or an experimental film, we allow ourselves to use the very same judgement that a man would have used two thousand years ago. It is this split, this break between what is new and this outdated sort of judgement that causes the whole thing to be regarded with suspicion.

Some days ago I read an interview with René Clair, in which the old master inveighed against his young colleagues today with his usual hard, glittering intelligence, accusing them of bad faith, stupidity and presumptuousness. His voice seemed to be that of good sense and truth and it was hard to remain unconvinced by his arguments.

And yet, if I were to be asked the same questions I should not know what to say, I should be quite bewildered. Perhaps those growing up around us - and all their manifestations, including their artistic manifestations - are so different from us and our work, so unrecognisable, that the natural respect felt for anything impossible

155

to evaluate should make us withhold judgement, or anyway should prompt us to give up our old points of reference and try to find new ones more suited to the new context.

In conclusion, it seems to me that what deludes and irritates us in the cinema, in literature and the theatre and in the figurative arts, is the limitedness of what they produce. A remarkable sort of limitedness which condemns no-one, not even the authors that express it, but rather shows how today's people are more individual, and culturally, spiritually and socially more evolved than they were. Until now, artists have always been the high points that burst out of a shapeless, passive mass, the common denominator in which others recognised themselves and from which they drew nourishment. Today, this denominator is rather less common because the more highly developed personality of each individual limits and reduces it, and the high points do not burst out at so high a level because the average, in the mass of people, is higher than it was. Whether this is a good thing or a bad thing, I don't know. Perhaps we are destined to become a whole human race of artists, each producing and nourishing himself on what he produces. Perhaps art, in the sense we know it, will no longer be necessary. These are utopian ideas, of course; but one thing we ought to bear in mind. We tend to say that men are the same and will always be the same, but what we really know about men goes back only 10,000 years. If you consider that the human race is millions of years old and will go on for as many million more, then every judgement, every assertion and every forecast is lost in the mists of time.

15. I have always thought that the cinema is a means of expression, an entirely original language that owes nothing, and bears no relationship, to any other art form. As far as literature is concerned, admittedly the cinema has borrowed a good deal from it, but this can be counted as normal interdependence between the arts. More important is the fact that whenever a literary work is godmother to a film, the result is always mediocre, disappointing and entirely to the disadvantage of the film. This may be the definite proof of the cinema's originality, showing that it cannot bear graftings or overlappings of any kind. Everything that connects the cinema with literature is the result of laziness and sentimental whim, when it is not actually due to brutal calculation. It is a case of doing something arbitrary and unnatural, like sticking four car wheels on to a horse, or cutting a steak into the shape of a cod-fish.

156

16. I feel that decadence is indispensable to rebirth. I have already said that I love shipwrecks. So I am happy to be living at a time when everything is capsizing. It's a marvellous time, for the very reason that a whole series of ideologies, concepts and conventions is being wrecked. Man went to the moon, didn't he? Well then, to keep talking of iron curtains, frontiers and different currencies is completely absurd. We've got to overthrow all that.

This process of dissolution is quite natural, I think. I don't see it as a sign of the death of civilisation but, on the contrary, as a sign of its life. It is the end of a certain phase of the human race. But the process of dissolution is too slow and must be hurried. We must start from scratch. Make a clean sweep of everything.

Is our society waiting for what is going to happen to it? Not at all. Force of circumstances causes society itself to generate what happens. There's no solution and no continuity . . . The young are aware that a new world is beginning. But it is very hard to speak of this without becoming rhetorical. The dawn which is coming moves me.

17. As a man I am interested in everything, and as far as what you call problems are concerned I go in search of them, because I am curious, and anxious to learn. But as a film director, I am quite indifferent to abstract problems, those which are now called ideological. For an idea or a situation or an atmosphere to kindle my mind or my imagination, to amuse me or to move me, it must come to me as a concrete fact. This may be a certain person or character that comes out to meet me; it may be the memory of a particular adventure or of a particular coincidence of human beings in a landscape or a situation. Then my imagination is kindled. If I were a composer I would then start writing down notes, if I were a painter I would scribble on the canvas. As a film director, I find my means of expression in the film image. I am a story-teller in the cinema and I can't honestly see what other qualification can be attributed to me apart from this - which may seem modest but, to me, is terribly demanding.

18. I believe - please note, I am only supposing - that what I care about most is the freedom of man, the liberation of the individual man from the network of moral and social convention in which he believes, or rather in which he thinks he believes, and which encloses him and limits him and makes him seem narrower, smaller, sometimes even worse than he really is. If you really want me to turn teacher, then condense it with these words: be what you are, that is, discover yourself, in order to love life. To me, life is beautiful, for all its tragedy and suffering, I like it, I enjoy it, I am moved by it. And I do my best to share this way of feeling with others.

19. Every period of stolid materialism is followed by times of spirituality. We are now living in a kind of dark tunnel of suffering, unable to communicate with one another, but I already feel I can see a gleam in the distance, a sense of new freedom: we must try to believe in this possibility of salvation.

20. If I say that I am fairly confident, I don't want to seem like a butterfly flitting carelessly from flower to flower, but like a person who feels alive, who has not yet exhausted his human adventure. Really, I like everything about life, and sometimes I feel electric with curiosity, as if I had not yet been fully born. Yes, I haven't yet lost faith in the journey, even though it often seems dark and desperate.

The important thing for man today is to hang on, not to let his head droop but to keep looking up along the tunnel, perhaps even inventing a way of salvation through fantasy or will-power, and especially through faith. For this reason I think that the work of artists is really needed today.

The birth of a film

A film cannot be described in words. If I talk about it, it becomes
a kind of materialisation that has nothing to do with the film itself.
If a film is born out of verbal images in those who are going to see
it, then it will be born preconstituted, outside its own nature.
Besides, I don't even know myself if it resembles what I wanted to
do. I have now hidden it within me, I have made it a secret.

A changeable, shifting thing. The first time it appears it is cloudy,
vague and indistinct. Any contact one has with it is in the imagination: it is a nocturnal sort of contact. It may be, indeed it is, a
friendly contact. At this point the film seems to have everything,
it seems to be entirely itself, whereas in fact it is nothing. It is a
vision, a feeling. What fascinates is its purity.

Then comes the second phase. The pure image gives place to
something quite hair-raising. The contract comes into being, involv-
ing lawyers and handshakes. Coca-cola is drunk, and toasts in
champagne. There's the statutory Roman atmosphere which
everyone knows and is reproduced each time with loathsome
exactness. The Americans turn up, and stay at the Grand Hotel.
One goes along and talks to them. They wander round the room
in underpants, grumpy, dyspeptic, avaricious: and while they're
talking to you, they ring up Tokyo. More drinking, more toasts.
The film shows a nastier, seamier side; yet a seductive one. It's
going to make money for you, which is something. Behind the
contract there's a cheque: fine, fine.

159

Fellini during the shooting of *Satyricon*

But then comes the third phase: the screenplay. This is the moment in which the film looms up and recedes at the same time. The screenplay acts as a detective, finding out what it will or may be like. One tries to see how it may be made more concrete. The first images appear very clearly, stimulated by nothing at all: they are attempts and excuses which cannot be seen for what they are. Then these images drift away: the screenplay has to be written, it has a literary rhythm, and the literary rhythm is quite different, it cannot be compared with the cinematic rhythm.

Before I worked on films of my own, I wrote a great many screenplays. It was work I found distressing. Words are seductive, but they flatten out the precise dimensions, the merely visual demands of the film.

In this third phase, the film seems to be pulled along by the hair, and puts up some resistance. It has to be persuaded in some way. Sometimes I expand the literary part in full consciousness of my bad faith, at others I leave pages and pages blank. Words bring more images to birth, and alter the end which the cinematic imagination envisages. Here one must stop, and in good time.

Meantime, the film is either glinting or else lies buried. But when the screenplay has been finished, it goes into a sort of limbo. For me this is the happiest phase: the phase when all possibilities, all unknown chances, are open to it. It may become something completely different from what it suggested beforehand. It is a matter of finding the faces from which it will live.

(At this stage, I get my 'eternal student' complex, and wish it may never end.)

I ought to be paid, and paid a very great deal, for the effort I make in this selection procedure. At this point I wish I could see all the faces on this planet. I am never satisfied, and even when I seem to be I still want to compare the face that satisfies me with others, with all possible faces. I am quite neurotic about it.

In the screenplay I may have written that a smile should be 'cutting': by rejecting this or that, I discover that the smile, instead of being 'cutting', is to be 'soft'. I have found a 'soft' smile that will wound a great deal more, in the image, than any smile which merely 'cuts'.

As I continue to seek among strangers for the faces, bodies and movements I need, the film begins to exist as it has not done so far. It exists at its most fascinating phase: in flashes, in bits and

161

pieces. And I find that I am greedily ready to let myself be seduced by these flashes and pieces: even by the hundred different, opposing ways of behaving, which a single character may be faced with.

In those little offices where the choice is made - wines, liqueurs, cigarette smoke, the whole ramshackle air always found in such places - in those little offices the most authentic propitiatory rite takes place around that vague, indistinct form which now begins to take on a visible, palpable physiognomy.

But the joy very soon vanishes. A collision with the production schedule's notice-board takes place. On this notice-board everything is planned and decided unnervingly in advance, and this makes every sort of fantasy vanish. We are now in February. On the coloured board I see that on May 7th I will be at Number 5 Studio to shoot 'The Port of Rimini'. There's no escape: I've got to be there. And I, who would like to take my vagueness and insecurity along with me, and my wish to change and dream, cannot avoid finding myself, neat and tidy, at Studio Number 5 on that date.

So I begin wandering from studio to studio, looking at the sets they are building. Indifferent workmen are busy with the things I have imagined. Everything is losing its allusiveness . . .

This need the film has to turn itself into something exact, into something that follows a particular rhythm and time-table, makes me lose all confidence in it. And the film loses all confidence in me, because I loathe these time-tables.

I am now up against the production people, trying to salvage something that belongs to me and no longer to the film. The film, now, has changed into a financial operation which the production people defend tooth and nail; and the film itself gives up the struggle. I am on this side, defending the origins from which I have seen it born, with all the imprecision and oddity that obviously governed it. I have my own algebra; the producers, and the film itself, reject this algebra. Hence grudges, rage, flight, illness, all of which must be endured.

What have I left? For my part, I have all the right superstitions and rituals: I have conceded everything to my childish instincts. When suspicion is at its height, chance sees to it that the first day's work comes along. No-one knows what's happening; then, after a few weeks, the whole business shows signs of gratitude.

Gratitude. That's it. At a certain point you realise that the film has begun to direct you, and that its algebra has become the same

162

as yours: it too has decided to invent itself, step by step. In all this, groups and friendships have been formed and have come out into the open. The life of a team making a film is a long journey made by a hundred people together: all sorts of things are happening around a framework. And the framework is nourished on all this, and abandons all else.

Then the film is finished. But it's a few days before the retakes are really done with. One day you realise you care nothing for that whirligig of marvels, the set. You go into a studio that has been yours, and find another team there, and another set being built: their alien presence seems like an intrusion, a violation. This is how the work ends - in a dispersal and an unravelling. But soon something turns up that seems like a new beginning. This is the first phase with the moviola. The relationship with the film becomes private and personal: I have to be alone with it and the editor.

On the set I like working among people: there, I have no need, as some people have, of an atmosphere of discipline and silence. I like people to come in and see me, and I indulge my taste for clowning. But in the cutting-room I won't have anyone. It is an operating theatre, and the object, the film, needs to be respected: it is nourished on itself.

Thus I come to the first personal vision. The film comes out of the moviola's small screen and goes on to the normal-sized screen. The images are its own, those it has managed to earn for itself and those with which I followed it. Around those images there is the untouched sound-track: the ragged noises of life on the set, shouts swearing, laughter, and silences obtained with difficulty. Its face is halfway between that of a blackmailer and a brother. Half an umbilical cord still holds us together: I have to cut it.

At this point I start to go away, to avoid the film, no longer to like looking it in the face. The magma from which I wished to drag it has fallen away, and my interest, too, is quickly melting away.

I finish it. Of course I finish it: always more pedantically, to separate myself from it more and more. But there is no longer any question of the earlier sense of awkward friendliness, or difficult loyalty.

Each phase, following upon another, alters the film more and more. Each time I see it, it is different: sometimes afflicted with neuroses, sometimes half paralysed, sometimes unworthy.

In the end I hand it over to its fate with a sense of ennui. I have

163

never seen a film of mine again in a public cinema. I am assailed by a sort of modesty; I find myself in the position of someone who doesn't want to see a friend of his do things he doesn't approve of.

It is impertinent to call my films autobiographical. I have invented my own life. I have invented it specifically for the screen. Before I directed my first film I did nothing but prepare myself to become tall enough and big enough and to charge myself with all the energy I needed to come to the point, one day, of saying 'Action!' I lived to discover and create a film director: no more. And I can remember nothing else, although I am thought to be a man whose whole expressive life is spent in the great department stores of memory.

In my films there is nothing in the form of anecdotes, or of autobiography. Instead, they bear witness to a certain time I have lived through. In that sense, yes, they are autobiographical: but only in the way that every book, every poem, every painting, is autobiographical.

None of what they say is true. I cannot have too many illusions about myself nor do I really want to have them.

I cannot distinguish my films one from another. For myself, I've always directed the same film. It is a matter of images and images only which I have directed, using the same materials, perhaps urged on, sometimes, from varying points of view.

What I know is that I want to tell stories. I am not saying this out of modesty, but simply because telling stories seems to me the only game worth playing. It is a game which makes its own demands on me, on my imagination and my nature. When I am playing it I feel free, away from all embarrassment. And I am lucky in this, that I can play with that toy, the cinema.

The dark set, when all the lights are out, exerts a fascination over me which has some very obscure origin. To put up some of the scenery with my own hands, to make up an actor, to dress him, to urge him to some movement, to some unforeseeable reaction, involves me totally, sucks out all my energies.

I know the unreality of it all: its limitations, the feeling of exaltation and extravagance which it brings, the dangerous romantic risks, but outside the cinema I know no other way in which I can feel at ease, and in tune with my own self.

Where should I shelter? What code of conduct should I obey?

Style is light. Light comes before everything, even before the plot, the screenplay or the word, as Leo Pestelli has said. Style is light, as in painting. Painting and the cinema are closely connected.

The film camera shows the distance between the film-maker and things, and helps to compose his style; although, with its movements, it acts rather as grammar does in writing, to regulate what is said.

As far as my own films are concerned, I move the camera very little. As I believe in expression, what matters is the way the space is cut up, the precision of what happens within the magical space of the frame, where I refuse to allow the smallest clumsiness. I become furious if there is a wrong movement, or a bad patch of lighting.

I am sure that the cinema does not allow one to be casual. Admittedly, there is a certain aesthetic school that believes in the most obvious casualness. What actually happens, though, is that the cinema takes advantage of its audience's ignorance.

If you bring a good cameraman, a good scriptwriter and a good actor together, you are bound to turn up something quite passable. But the result is a cobbling together, which is all that this casualness can achieve. There is a type of film director who broods over all this; and the more humble and modest he is, the more people are generous towards him.

I am certain that a completely different method of working is needed. On the vague, cloudy, uncertain film, as it is first found in the director's imagination, he must act rigorously. I believe in light, and light is what I use, what my imagination needs. My light will never be sunlight. I believe in constructing daylight, and even the sea, in a studio.

In *Amarcord*, I built the sea. And nothing is truer than that sea on the screen. It is the sea I wanted, which the real sea would never have given me. How do you build the sea? That's a trade secret I would not want to reveal. A couple of sheets of plastic and a couple of good-natured operators, and you have it. I work for this, to be there, to cut and nail, paint and set up lights. The cinema is an illusion: an image that must emerge for what it is.

I make a film as if I were escaping, as if I had to avoid an illness. I choose to direct, or come to direct on the set, when I am overcome by hatred, when I am full of bitterness. It is a creation inspired by dislike. I do all that is necessary pedantically, then more and

165

more pedantically; I am seized by a kind of disgusted rage. In the end I have to move away from the film, and if I didn't, it would be all the worse.

I should prefer not to talk about it. But talking about the film one has just made is part of a commercial ritual from which it is impossible to be free. The press officers get going, the telephone starts up, and it is just like standing in front of a mirror. But one ought to be silent.

Yet I love all the rumbustiousness of the cinema, and I thrive on it. But with my own films, with each one of my films, I have never had a good relationship. Our relationship is one of mutual dislike.

I feel like a criminal. I want to leave no traces of what a film has cost me. I destroy everything. All that must be left is the film, bare and finished. In the same way I dislike making confessions.

Now I've seen this blessed film of mine. And it's something like my own nature. And yet . . .

Filmography

Early Biography

Born in Rimini on 20 January 1920. Father: Urbano Fellini, a
travelling salesman from Savignano. Mother: Ida Barbiani, from
Rome. A brother: Riccardo. A sister: Maddalena. Aged ten,
Federico runs away from home and joins Pierino's circus, where
he looks after a sick zebra. During the war he travels all over Italy
with a touring theatre troupe, writing sketches for them. After a
period in Florence, he moves to Rome, where he writes and does
drawings for the humorous weekly, 'Marc Aurelio', works on
comics as an illustrator and translator, writes radio plays and is
gag-writer for the comedian Macario. In the course of his work for
radio he gets to know Giulietta Masina, whom he marries in Rome
on 30 October 1943. They have a son in the summer of 1944 who
dies when only a few weeks old. With the arrival of the American
forces Fellini opens his 'Funny Face Shop' where he draws
caricatures and portrait sketches of the soldiers. It is here that
Rossellini meets him in 1945 and takes him on as assistant on
Roma, città aperta.

Fellini's films have been awarded the following major prizes:
the Silver Lion of Venice for *I vitelloni* (1953) and *La strada*
(1954); Oscars for the best foreign film for *La strada* (1956),
Le notti di Cabiria (1957) and *Amarcord* (1975); Oscar for the
best direction for *8½* (1963); the Golden Palm of Cannes for
La dolce vita (1963); and the Grand Prix of Moscow for *8½* (1963).

Films as writer, assistant or collaborator.

1940-
44   Gag-writer on comedian Macario's first films (director:
Mario Mattoli): *Il pirata sono io*; *Non me lo dire*; *Lo vedi
come sei?*
Co-writer and assistant to the directors (Alfredo Guarini,
Mario Bonnard, Nicola Manzari, Goffredo Alessandrini)
on: *Avanti c'è posto*; *Campo dei Fiori*; *L'ultima carrozzella*;
Documento Z3; *Quarta pagina*; *Chi l'ha visto?*

1945   Assistant to Rossellini on *Roma, città aperta.*

1946   Collaborator (story, screenplay, dialogue, direction) with
Rossellini on *Paisà.* Co-writer on Alberto Lattuada's *Il
delitto di Giovanni Episcopo.*

1947   Co-author, with Tullio Pinelli, of the screenplay of
Alberto Lattuada's *Senza pietà.*

1948   Author, assistant director, screenplaywright and actor in
Rossellini's *Il miracolo*, which together with *Una voce
umana* made up the film *L'amore.* Assistant to Pietro
Germi on *In nome della legge.*

1949   Assistant to Alberto Lattuada on *Il mulino del Po.*
Screenplaywright and assistant to Rossellini on *Francesco,
giullare di Dio.*

1950   Assistant to Pietro Germi on *Il cammino della speranza.*

1951   Brief participation on Rossellini's *Europa 51.* Assistant
to Pietro Germi on *La città si difende.*

1952   Assistant to Pietro Germi on *Il brigante di Tacca del
Lupo.*

1958   Screenplaywright on Eduardo De Filippo's *Fortunella.*

Films as director.

1950   LUCI DEL VARIETA (Variety Lights). *Producers*: Fellini
and Alberto Lattuada for Capitolium Film. *Directors*:
Alberto Lattuada and Fellini. *Story*: Fellini. *Screenplay*:
Fellini, Alberto Lattuada, Tullio Pinelli, Ennio Flaiano.
Photography: Otello Martelli. *Production designer*: Aldo
Buzzi. *Music*: Felice Lattuada. *Editor*: Mario Bonotti.
Cast: Peppino De Filippo (*Checco Dalmonte*), Carla Del
Poggio (*Liliana*), Giulietta Masina (*Melina*), John Kitzmiller,
Folco Lulli, Franca Valeri, Carlo Romano, Silvio Bagolini,
Dante Maggio, Gina Mascetti, Vittorio Caprioli, Alberto

Bonucci.

1952 LO SCEICCO BIANCO (The White Sheikh). *Producer*:
Enzo Provenzale. *Production Company*: Luigi Rovere
P.D.C./O.F.I. *Director*: Fellini. *Story*: Fellini, Michelangelo
Antonioni, Tullio Pinelli. *Screenplay*: Fellini, Tullio
Pinelli, Ennio Flaiano. *Photography*: Arturo Gallea.
Music: Nino Rota. *Editor*: Rolando Benedetti.
Cast: Brunella Bovo (*Wanda*), Leopoldo Trieste (*Ivan
Cavalli*), Alberto Sordi (*the White Sheikh*), Giulietta
Masina (*Cabiria*), Fanny Marchio (*Marliena Velardi*),
Ernesto Almirante, Enzo Maggio, Lilia Lanci, Gina
Mascetti.

1953 I VITELLONI (The Layabouts). *Production Company*:
Peg Film, Cité Films. *Director*: Fellini. *Story*: Fellini,
Tullio Pinelli. *Screenplay*: Fellini, Ennio Flaiano, Tullio
Pinelli. *Photography*: Otello Martelli, assisted by Luciano
Trasatti, Carlo Carlini. *Production designer*: Mario Chiari.
Music: Nino Rota. *Editor*: Rolando Benedetti.
Cast: Franco Interlenghi (*Moraldo*), Alberto Sordi
(*Alberto*), Franco Fabrizi (*Fausto*), Leopoldo Trieste
(*Leopoldo*), Riccardo Fellini (*Riccardo*), Eleonora Ruffo
(*Sandra*), Jean Brochard (*Fausto's father*), Claude Farell
(*Alberto's sister*), Carlo Romano (*Signore Michele*),
Enrico Viarisio (*Sandra's father*), Paola Borboni (*Sandra's
mother*), Lida Baarova (*Signora Michele*), Arlette Sauvage
(*woman in the cinema*), Vira Silenti (*little Chinawoman*),
Maja Nipora (*soubrette*), Achille Majeroni, Guido Martufi,
Silvio Bagolini, Milvia Chianelli, Franca Gandolfi.

1953 UN' AGENZIA MATRIMONIALE (A Matrimonial Agency).
[A sketch for the film *L'amore in città*, the other episodes
coming from Michelangelo Antonioni, Dino Risi, Cesare
Zavattini and Francesco Maselli, Alberto Lattuada, Carlo
Lizzani (his sketch was cut by the censor).] *Production
Company*: Faro Film. *Director*: Fellini. *Story and screen-
play*: Fellini, Tullio Pinelli. *Photography*: Gianni di
Venanzo. *Production designer*: Gianni Polidoro. *Music*:
Mario Nascimbene. *Editor*: Eraldo da Roma.
Cast: Amateurs, some from the Centro Sperimentale di
Cinematografia.

1954 LA STRADA. *Production Company*: Carlo Ponti - Dino
De Laurentiis. *Director*: Fellini, Tullio Pinelli. *Screenplay*:

Fellini, Ennio Flaiano, Tullio Pinelli. *Dialogue*: Tullio
Pinelli. *Photography*: Otello Martelli. *Production designer*:
Mario Ravasco. *Costumes*: Marinari. *Music*: Nino Rota.
Editor: Leo Catozzo.
Cast: Giulietta Masina (*Gelsomina*), Anthony Quinn
(*Zampanò*), Richard Basehart (*Il Matto*), Aldo Silvani
(*Mr. Giraffe*), Marcella Rovere (*widow*), Lidia Venturini
(*the little nun*)

1955   IL BIDONE (The Swindlers). *Production Company*:
Titanus. *Director*: Fellini. *Story and screenplay*: Fellini,
Tullio Pinelli, Ennio Flaiano. *Photography*: Otello Martelli.
Production designer: Dario Cecchi. *Music*: Nino Rota.
Editors: Mario Serandrei, Giuseppe Vari. *Artistic adviser*:
Brunello Rondi.
Cast: Broderick Crawford (*Augusto*), Richard Basehart
(*Picasso*), Franco Fabrizi (*Roberto*), Giulietta Masina
(*Iris*), Xenia Valderi, Alberto de Amicis, Lorella de Luca,
Sue Ellen Blake, Maria Werlen, Giacomo Gabrielli, Irene
Cefaro, Riccardo Garrone, Paul Greuter, Emilio Manfredi,
Mario Passante, Maria Zanoli, Lucetta Muratori, Sara
Simoni, Ettore Bevilacqua.

1957   LE NOTTI DI CABIRIA (Cabiria). *Production Company*:
Dino De Laurentiis. *Director*: Fellini. *Story and screenplay*:
Fellini, Ennio Flaiano, Tullio Pinelli. *Adaptation of the
dialogue into Romagnan dialect*: Pier Paolo Pasolini.
Photography: Aldo Tonti, Otello Martelli. *Production
designer*: Piero Gherardi. *Music*: Nino Rota. *Editor*:
Leo Catozzo.
Cast: Giulietta Masina (*Cabiria*), Amadeo Nazzari (*the
actor*), Francois Périer (*D'Onofrio*), Aldo Silvani (*the
hypnotist*), Franca Marzi (*Wanda*), Dorian Gray (*Jessy*),
Mario Passante, Ennio Girolami, Christian Tassou.

1959   LA DOLCE VITA. *Producer*: Giuseppe Amato for Riama
Film/Pathé Consortium Cinéma. *Director*: Fellini. *Story*:
Fellini, Ennio Flaiano, Tullio Pinelli, Brunello Rondi.
Production designer: Piero Gherardi. *Photography*: Otello
Martelli. *Camera operator*: Arturo Zavattini. *Music*: Nino
Rota. *Editor*: Leo Catozzo. *Special effects*: Otello Fava.
Make-up: Renata Magnanti. *Sound*: Agostino Moretti.
Cast: Marcello Mastroianni (*Marcello Rubini*), Walter
Santesso (*Paparazzo*), Anouk Aimée (*Maddalena*),

Yvonne Fourneaux (*Emma*), Anita Ekberg (*Sylvia*), Lex
Barker (*Robert*), Adriano Celentano (*rock'n'roll singer*),
Alan Dijon (*Frankie Stout*), Alain Cuny (*Steiner*), Valeria
Ciangottini (*Paola*), Renée Longarini (*Signora Steiner*),
Annibale Ninchi (*Marcello's father*), Polidor (*clown*),
Magali Noël (*Fanny*), Giulio Questi (*Don Giulio Mascalchi*),
Nadia Gray (*Nadia*), Mino Doro (*Nadia's lover*), Jacques
Sernas (*the filmstar*), Laura Betti (*singer and actress*),
Daniela Calvino (*Daniela*), Riccardo Garrone (*host*),
Enrico Glori (*Nadia's admirer*), Mario Conocchia (*man
with bra on his head*).

1961   LE TENTAZIONI DEL DOTTOR ANTONIO (The
Temptations of Doctor Antonio). [Episode from *Boccaccio
'70*; the other episodes directed by Luchino Visconti,
Vittorio de Sica, Mario Monicelli.] *Producer*: Carlo Ponti.
Director: Fellini. *Story and Screenplay*: Fellini, Ennio
Flaiano, Tullio Pinelli (in collaboration with Brunello
Rondi and Goffredo Parise). *Colour photography*: Otello
Martelli. *Production designer*: Piero Zuffi. *Music*: Nino
Rota. *Editor*: Leo Catazzo.
Cast: Peppino De Filippo (*Dr. Antonio Mazzuolo*), Anita
Ekberg (*Anita*), Antonio Acqua (*The Pope*), Donatella
Della Nora (*Mazzuolo's sister*), Monique Berger.

1962   8½. *Producer*: Angelo Rizzoli. *Director*: Fellini. *Story*:
Fellini, Ennio Flaiano. *Screenplay*: Fellini, Tullio Pinelli,
Ennio Flaiano, Brunello Rondi. *Photography*: Gianni di
Vananzo. *Camera operator*: Pasquale de Santis. *Production
designer*: Piero Gherardi. *Music*: Nino Rota. *Special effects*:
Otello Fava. *Editor*: Leo Catozzo.
Cast: Marcello Mastroianni (*Guido*), Anouk Aimée (*Luisa,
Guido's wife*), Sandra Milo (*Carla, Guido's mistress*), Edra
Gale (*Saraghina*), Claudia Cardinale (*Claudia*), Jean
Rougeul (*Carini*), Tito Masini (*the cardinal*), Ian Dallas
(*Maurice, the telepathist*), Rossella Falk (*Rossella*),
Annibale Ninchi (*Guido's father*), Giuditta Rissone (*Guido's
mother*), Mario Pisu (*Mezzabotta*), Barbara Steel (*Gloria
Morin*), Guido Alberti (*Pace, the producer*), Madeleine
Lebeau (*French actress*), Caterina Boratto (*vision of the
beautiful stranger*).

1965   GIULIETTA DEGLI SPIRITI. (Juliet of the Spirits).
Producer: Angelo Rizzoli. *Director*: Fellini. *Story*: Fellini,

Tullio Pinelli. *Screenplay*: Fellini, Ennio Flaiano, Tullio
Pinelli, Brunello Rondi. *Colour Photography*: Gianni di
Vananzo. *Camera Operator*: Pasquale de Santis. *Production
designer*: Piero Gherardi. *Music*: Nino Rota. *Special effects*:
Otello Fava, Eligio Trani. *Editor*: Ruggero Mastroianni.
Cast: Giulietta Masina (*Giulietta*), Mario Pisu (*Giorgio,
Giulietta's husband*), Sandra Milo (*Susy, Iris, dancer*),
Lou Gilbert (*grandfather*), Caterina Boratto (*Giulietta's
mother*), Luisa della Noce (*Adele*), Sylvia Koscina (*Silva*),
Alba Cancellieri (*Giulietta as a child*), Friedrich Ledebur
(*schoolmaster, hermit*), Valentina Cortese (*Valentina*),
Silvana Jachino (*Dolly*), Valeska Gert (*Bhishma*), José de
Villalonga (*José*), Mario Conocchia (*Connocchia*).

1968   TOBY DAMMIT. [Episode from *Histoires Extraordinaires*
(Tales of Mystery); the other episodes directed by Louis
Malle (*William Wilson*) and Roger Vadim (*Metzengerstein*).]
Production company: Les Films Marceau/Cocinor (Paris)/
P.E.A. Cinematografica (Rome). *Director*: Fellini.
Screenplay: Fellini, Bernardino Zapponi, based on the story
Never Bet the Devil Your Head by Edgar Allan Poe. *Music*:
Nino Rota. *Colour Photography*: Giuseppe Rotunno.
Editor: Ruggero Mastroianni. *Art direction*: Pierro Tosi.
Cast: Terence Stamp (*Toby Dammit*), Salvo Randone,
Anna Tonietti, Fabrizio Angeli, Ernesto Colli, Marina
Yaru, Aleardo Ward, Paul Cooper, James Robertson.

1968   BLOCK-NOTES DI UN REGISTA (A Director's Notebook).
Production company: N.B.C. *Producer*: Peter Goldfarb.
Director: Fellini. *Screenplay*: Fellini, Bernadino Zapponi.
Colour photography: Pasquale de Santis. *Assistant
directors*: Maurizio Mein, Liliana Betti. *Dialogue director*:
Christopher Cruise. *English dialogue*: Eugene Walter.
Music: Nino Rota. *Editor*: Ruggero Mastroianni.
Cast: Giulietta Masina, Marcello Mastroianni, Caterina
Boratto, Marina Boratto, David Maunsell, Professor
Genius, Cesarino.

1969   FELLINI SATYRICON. *Production company*: P.E.A.
(Rome)/Les Productions Artistes Associés (Paris).
Producer: Alberto Grimaldi. *Director*: Fellini. *Screenplay*:
Fellini, Bernardino Zapponi, freely adapted from *Satyricon*
by Petronius Arbiter. *Colour Photography*: Giuseppe
Rotunno. *Camera operator*: Giuseppe Maccari. *Production

172

designer: Danilo Donati. *Art direction*: Luigi Scaccianoce, based on sketches by Fellini. *Make-up*: Rino Carboni. *Music*: Nino Rota, Ilhan Mimaroglu. *Special effects*: Adriano Pischiutta. *Editor*: Ruggero Mastroianni.
Cast: Martin Potter (*Encolpius*), Hiram Keller (*Ascyltus*), Max Born (*Giton*), Mario Romagnoli (*Trimalchio*), Fanfulla (*Vernacchio*), Gordon Mitchell (*robber*), Capucine (*Tryphaena*), Donyale Luna (*Enothea*), Salvo Randone (*Eumolpus*), Lucia Bose (*suicide wife*), Joseph Wheeler (*suicide husband*), Alain Cuny (*Lichas*), Tanya Lopert (*Imperator*), Magali Noël (*Fortunata*), Hylette Adolphe (*oriental slave girl*), Silvio Belusci (*dwarf*), Pasquale Fasciano (*magician*), Patricia Hartley (*magician's assistant*), Sibilla Sedat (*nymphomaniac*), Lorenzo Piani (*nymphomaniac's husband*), Luigi Zerbatini (*nymphomaniac's slave*), Genaro Sabatino (*ferryman*), Pasquale Baldassare (*hermaphrodite*), Antonia Petrosi (*widow of Ephesus*), Danika La Loggia (*Scintilla*), Giuseppe San Vitale (*Habinnas*), Luigi Montefiori (*Minotaur*), Marcello Bifolco (*Proconsul*), Carlo Giordana (*captain*), Genius [Eugenio Mastropietro] (*Cinedo*).

1970   I CLOWNS (The Clowns). *Production company*: R.A.I./ Leone (Rome)/O.R.T.F. (Paris)/Bavaria Film (Munich). *Producers*: Elio Scardimaglia, Ugo Guerra, Fellini. *Screenplay*: Fellini, Bernardino Zapponi. *Colour photography*: Dario di Palma. *Art direction*: Danilo Donati. *Assistant director*: Maurizio Mein. *Music*: Nino Rota. *Editor*: Ruggero Mastroianni.
Cast: *Italian Clowns*: Billi, Scotti, Fanfulla, Rizzo, Pistani, Furia, Sbarra Carini, Carini, Terzo, Vingelli, Fumagalli, Zerbinati, Reder, Valentini, Merli, The 4 Colombaioni, The Martanas, Maggio, Janigro, Maunsel, Peverello, Sorrentino, Valdemaro, Bevilacqua. *French Clowns*: Alex, Père Loriot, Maïss, Bario, Ludo, Charlie Rivel, Nino. *The T.V. Troupe*: Maya Morin, Lina Alberti, Alvaro Vitali, Gasperino. *Others*: Liana Orfei, Rinaldo Orfei, Nando Orfei, Franco Miglierini, Anita Ekberg, Pierre Etaix, Annie Fratellini, Victor Fratellini, Baptiste, Tristan Rémy, Victoria Chaplin, Fellini.

1971   ROMA (Fellini's Roma). *Production company*: Ultra Film (Rome)/Les Artistes Associés (Paris). *Producer*: Turi

Vasile. *Production manager*: Lamberto Pippia. *Director*:
Fellini. *Story and screenplay*: Fellini, Bernardino Zapponi.
Colour Photography: Giuseppe Rotunno. *Production
designer*: Danilo Donati. *Music*: Nino Rota. *Choreography*:
Gino Landi. *Assistant directors*: Maurizio Mein, Paolo
Pietrangeli, Tonino Antonucci. *Special effects*: Rino
Carboni. *Editor*: Ruggero Mastroianni.
Cast: Peter Gonzales (*Federico Fellini at 18*), Britta
Barnes, Pia de Dores, Fiona Florence, Marne Maitland,
Renato Giovannoli, Elisa Mainard, Paule Rout, Galliano
Sbarra, Paolo Natale, Marcelle Ginette Bron, Mario del
Vago, Alfredo Adami, Stefano Mayore; *with*: Fellini,
Alberto Sordi, Marcello Mastroianni, Anna Magnani,
Gore Vidal.

1973 AMARCORD. *Production company*: F.C. Produzioni
(Rome)/P.E.C.F. (Paris). *Producer*: Franco Cristaldi.
Director: Fellini. *Story and screenplay*: Fellini, Tonino
Guerra. *Colour Photography*: Giuseppe Rotunno. *Camera
operators*: Giuseppe Maccari, Massimo di Venanzo,
Roberto Aristarco. *Assistant directors*: Maurizio Mein,
Liliana Betti, Nestore Baratella, Gerald Morin. *Production
designer*: Danilo Donati. *Music*: Nino Rota. *Special
effects*: Adriano Pischiutta, Rino Carboni. *Make-up*:
Amalia Paoletti. *Editor*: Ruggero Mastroianni.
Cast: Pupella Maggio (*Titta's mother*), Armando Brancia
(*Titta's father*), Bruno Zanin (*Titta*), Stefano Proietti
(*Oliva*), Peppino Ianigro (*grandfather*), Nando Orfei
(*Pataca*), Carla Mora (*maid*), Ciccio Ingrassia (*the lunatic
uncle*), Magali Noël (*Gradisca*), Luigi Rossi (*lawyer*), Maria
Antonietta Beluzzi (*tobacconist*), Josiane Tanzilli (*Volpina*),
Gennaro Ombra (*Biscein*), Gianfilippo Carcano (*Don
Balosa*), Aristide Caporale (*Giudizio*), Ferruccio Brembilla
(*Fascist leader*), Antonino Faa' di Bruno (*Conte di
Lovignano*), Gianfranco Marocco (*Conte Poltavo*), Alvaro
Vitali (*Naso*), Bruno Scagnetti (*Ovo*), Bruno Lenzi
(*Gigliozzi*), Fernando de Felice (*Ciccio*), Francesca Vona
(*Candela*), Donatella Gambini (*Aldina Cordini*), Franco
Magno (*headmaster*), Mauro Misul (*philosophy master*),
Armando Villella (*Professor Fighetta*), Dina Adorni
(*maths teacher*), Francesco Maselli (*physics master*),
Mario Silvestri (*Italian master*), Fides Stagni (*art teacher*),

Marcello Bonini Olas (*gym teacher*), Domenico Pertica
(*blindman*), Fausto Signoretti (*coachman*), Fredo Pistoni
(*Colonia*), Mario Nebolini (*town-clerk*), Vincenzo Caldarola
(*beggar/emir*), Mario Liberati (*owner of the Fulgor*),
Fiorella Magalotti (*Gradisca's sister*), Marina Trovalusci
(*Gradisca's sister when small*), Milo Mario (*photographer*),
Antonio Spaccatini (*Federale*), Bruno Bartocci (*Gradisca's
bridegroom*), Marco Laurentino, Riccardo Satta, Carmela
Eusepi, Clemente Baccherini, Marcello di Falco, Mario
del Vago.

List of sources

Rimini, my home town (Il mio paese) first appeared as the Introduction to 'La mia Rimini', edited by Renzo Renzi, published by Capelli, Bologna 1967.

Sweet beginnings first appeared in 'Segnacolo', Bologna, August 1961; the (anonymous) translation used here appeared in 'Atlas', New York, February 1962.

Miscellany I: nos. 1, 23, 29 from an interview with Lillian Ross, 'The New Yorker', New York, 30 Oct. 1965; no. 2 from 'Der Regisseur Federico Fellini', fifth contribution to the series 'Hervorragende Filmgestalter', edited by Rudolph S. Joseph, Photo- und Filmmuseum im Münchner Stadtmuseum, n.d.; nos. 3—8, 10—21, 26—28 from 'L'Arc', 45, Aix-en-Provence 1971; no. 9 from 'Noi e il telefono' by Fellini and Giulietta Masina, 'Le Firme de Selezionando', Turin, December 1972; no. 22 from the Preface to 'Henri de Toulouse-Lautrec', edited by Philippe Huisman and M. G. Dortu, published by Fratelli Fabbri, Milan 1971; nos. 24, 25 from 'Entretiens avec Federico Fellini', an interview with Dominique Delouche, 'Les Cahiers RTB, Série Télécinéma, published by Radiodiffusion Télévision Belge, Brussels 1962.

Letter to a Marxist critic: from 'Il Contemporaneo', No. 15, 9 April 1955.

Letter to a Jesuit priest: from 'Der Filmberater', No. 15, Zurich, September 1957 (translated from the Italian).

Via Veneto: dolce vita first appeared in 'L'Europeo', No. 27, Milan 1962.

176

Notes on censorship: from 'La Tribuna del Cinema', No. 2,
August 1958.
The bitter life - of money: from 'Films and Filming', London,
January 1961.
With 8½ in Moscow (Io a Mosca) first appeared in 'Panorama',
Milan, October 1963.
Miscellany II: nos. 1, 2, 12, 18, 33 from 'Entretiens avec Federico
Fellini', op. cit.; no. 3 from 'Positif', No. 76, Paris, June 1966;
nos. 4–6, 8, 9, 13–15, 22–24, 26, 31, 32 from 'L'Arc', 45, Aix-
en-Provence 1971; nos. 7, 19 from an interview with Callisto
Cosulich, 'ABC', Milan, 7 June 1964; no. 10 from the Preface to
the anthology 'The Art of Humorous Illustrations', Watson Guptill,
New York 1973; nos. 11, 16, 20 from 'Der Regisseur Federico
Fellini', op. cit.; no. 17 from an interview with Francesco Rigamonti,
'Amica', Milan, 30 Sept. 1962; nos. 21, 28 from the interview with
Lillian Ross already cited; no. 25 from 'Federico Fellini' by
Gilbert Salachas, Collection Cinéma d'aujourdhui No. 13,
published by Seghers, Paris 1970; no. 27 from a manuscript (in
Italian) in Fellini's possession; nos. 29, 30 from an essay by
Fellini in 'Il Resto del Carlino', Bologna, n.d.
Why clowns? (Un viaggio nell'ombra) first appeared in 'I Clowns',
edited by Renzo Renzi, published by Capelli, Bologna 1970.
Comic-strip heroes is taken from the manuscript of the Preface to
'History of Comics' by James Steranko, published by Super
Graphics, Reading, Penn. 1970 (translated from the Italian).
'Whom do you most admire?': reply to Renato Barneschi, 'Oggi
Illustrato', Milan, 12 Feb. 1972 (sections on Gradisca and Edgar
Wallace have been omitted as repeating material elsewhere in
the book, but the piece on Borges, originally left out of the 'Oggi'
article, has been added).
Miscellany III: nos. 1, 3 from a manuscript in Fellini's possession;
no. 2 in reply to a question from Université Radiophonique
Internationale, La Table Ronde, Paris, May 1960; nos. 4, 21 from
'L'Arc', 45, Aix-en-Provence 1971; nos. 5, 16 from an interview
in 'L'Express', Paris, 15 Sept. 1969; nos. 6, 7 from 'Etudes
Cinématographiques', No. 32–35, Paris 1964; no. 8 from 'Der
Regisseur Federico Fellini', op. cit.; nos. 9, 10 from 'Le Néo-
réalisme italien et ses créateurs' by Patrice G. Hovald, Collection
7e Art, Editions du Cerf, Paris 1959; no. 11 from the Preface to
'The Art of Humorous Illustrations', op. cit.; no. 12 from
'Entretiens avec Federico Fellini', op. cit.; no. 13 from a manu-

script in Fellini's possession, dated December 1972; nos. 14, 15 from a manuscript in Fellini's possession; nos. 17, 18 from an interview with Grazia Livi, 'Epoca', Milan, 11 Feb. 1962.
The birth of a film is based on a conversation with Enzo Siciliano in 'Il Mondo', Rome, 13 Sept. 1973.

Translators

Except where stated otherwise, pieces which appeared first in Italian or French have been translated for this edition by Isabel Quigly, and pieces which appeared first in German have been translated by Nicholas Hern. Those pieces which appeared first in English are reprinted without alteration.

Index

to film titles and stills